This study of John will help you slow down, hear God's voice, and walk away with a deeper love for Jesus.

Zach Windahl
Author and content creator

This study has done a remarkable job making one of the richest books in Scripture both approachable and transformative. Using their E.A.S.Y. method, Ashley, Taylor, and Ellen faithfully guide readers through the text while never losing sight of the worship and application it demands. Each week is thoughtfully divided into daily studies, giving you context, cross-references, and space to reflect, annotate, and respond. This theologically grounded study helps readers not only understand John's gospel but encounter the living Christ through it. If you've ever wanted to learn how to study Scripture faithfully *and* experience heart-level change, this resource makes it truly E.A.S.Y.

Faith Womack
Author of *No More Boring Bible Study* and Chief "Bible Nerd" at Bible Nerd Ministries

This book is a wonderful resource for those learning to study the Bible for the first time yet also packed full of wisdom for lifelong students of the Word. Perhaps what I love most is how Ashley, Taylor, and Ellen include visual example after visual example of how they personally highlight, color-code, and otherwise mark up the text of the Bible when studying it. Imitate them! These authors model the best kind of Bible study: at once rigorous, devotional, theological, and applicational. Buy yourself a copy of this book, then buy some more for your friends and get to know God better together!

Erik Lundeen
Assistant Academic Dean at Christ Our Redeemer Seminary, Auburn, AL

THE GOSPEL OF JOHN

A 7-WEEK STUDY

ASHLEY ARMIJO, TAYLOR MITCHELL, AND ELLEN KRAUSE

The Creators of *Coffee and Bible Time*

MOODY PUBLISHERS
CHICAGO

© 2025 by
Ashley Armijo, Taylor Mitchell, and Ellen Krause

All rights reserved. No part of this book may be reproduced in any form without permission in writing from the publisher, except in the case of brief quotations embodied in critical articles or reviews.

Scripture quotations are from the ESV® Bible (The Holy Bible, English Standard Version®), © 2001 by Crossway, a publishing ministry of Good News Publishers. Used by permission. All rights reserved. The ESV text may not be quoted in any publication made available to the public by a Creative Commons license. The ESV may not be translated in whole or in part into any other language.

Scripture quotations marked (NLT) are taken from the Holy Bible, New Living Translation, copyright ©1996, 2004, 2015 by Tyndale House Foundation. Used by permission of Tyndale House Publishers, Carol Stream, Illinois 60188. All rights reserved.

Names and details of some stories have been changed to protect the privacy of individuals.

Edited by Ashleigh Slater
Interior design: Puckett Smartt
Cover design: Brittany Schrock
Cover collage graphic copyright © 2025 by Oleksandra/Adobe Stock (462284695).
All rights reserved.
Authors photo: Isaac Mitchell

Library of Congress Cataloging-in-Publication Data

Names: Armijo, Ashley author | Krause, Taylor author | Krause, Ellen author

Title: The gospel of John : a 7-week study the easy Bible study method / Ashley Armijo, Taylor Krause, and Ellen Krause.
Description: Chicago : Moody Publishers, [2026] | Includes bibliographical references. | Summary: "Using The Easy Bible Study Method, the Coffee and Bible Time team walk us through one of the most beloved books of the Bible-the gospel of John. In this seven-week Bible study, readers dwell in John's gospel, learning how to Enter into stories, Assess the main ideas, Seek God and His character, and Yearn for heart change and deeper intimacy with Jesus"-- Provided by publisher.
Identifiers: LCCN 2025036573 (print) | LCCN 2025036574 (ebook) | ISBN 9780802434180 paperback | ISBN 9780802470898 ebook
Subjects: LCSH: Bible. John--Study and teaching | Bible. John--Criticism, interpretation, etc.
Classification: LCC BS2616 .A7325 2026 (print) | LCC BS2616 (ebook)
LC record available at https://lccn.loc.gov/2025036573
LC ebook record available at https://lccn.loc.gov/2025036574

Originally delivered by fleets of horse-drawn wagons, the affordable paperbacks from D. L. Moody's publishing house resourced the church and served everyday people. Now, after more than 125 years of publishing and ministry, Moody Publishers' mission remains the same—even if our delivery systems have changed a bit. For more information on other books (and resources) created from a biblical perspective, go to www.moodypublishers.com or write to:

Moody Publishers
820 N. LaSalle Boulevard
Chicago, IL 60610

1 3 5 7 9 10 8 6 4 2

Printed in Colombia

For our incredible husbands—
Johnny Armijo, Douglas Krause, and Isaac Mitchell—
your unwavering love, steady encouragement,
and constant belief in us made this possible.

We truly couldn't have done it without you.

Contents

Before Diving In

From Ashley, Taylor, and Ellen

Before we dive deep into studying the gospel of John, we want to introduce ourselves! This Bible study comes from the hearts of two sisters, Ashley and Taylor, and our mom, Ellen. The three of us do online ministry together at Coffee and Bible Time and love connecting with people all over the world and teaching them how to study the Bible. We have seen many benefits from the EASY Bible Study Method, and we are here to guide you through the process step by step. We are so excited to delve into God's Word with you! Let's get started!

Get to Know Us!

Scan to get to know us, or go to: coffeeandbibletime.com

This Bible Study Is for You

From Ashley, Taylor, and Ellen

The Bible is shallow enough for a child to wade in yet deep enough for an elephant to drown."[1] This statement couldn't be truer. A child can grasp the mystery that Jesus loves them, yet at the same time, scholars spend their entire lives studying the complexities of Scripture, never reaching its full depth.

The book of John is simple yet profound. Its central theme is about the good news of Jesus, who loves the world and loves you. It shares the clear story of God sending His Son into the world to live a perfect life, die the death we deserved, and rise again. Every word written is there for a purpose—"so that you may believe that Jesus is the Christ, the Son of God, and that by believing you may have life in his name" (John 20:31).

Each sentence in John is packed with meaning and depth. The book contains over a hundred connections to the Old Testament and many theological, historical, and cultural concepts. But, if this is your first Bible study or it has been a while since you've done one, we don't want you to be scared away by John's vastness. Studying Scripture does not have to feel overwhelming. It can be incredibly fulfilling, regardless of your background or experience.

So, if you need a place to start or restart, *this study is for you*! The goal of this study is to keep things simple. We will open our hearts to the profound truths of God's love and the heart of Jesus Himself. Not only will you learn how to study the Bible for yourself, but more importantly, you will encounter the God of the universe on every page, and your personal relationship with Him will grow as a result.

In this study, we will highlight important stories and key individuals whom Jesus encountered during His time on earth. These people are not much different than you and me. They are normal, regular, everyday people who Jesus called to Himself. As you get to know them, their stories, and how Jesus loved them, we hope that you will see that, just like them, God has called you to follow Jesus more deeply in faith and obedience. **He intentionally called you to believe in Him.** He continues to be after your heart and wants to see you grow in your relationship with Him and enjoy the benefits of eternal life now!

Here is the breakdown of **who you will encounter** as you read through seven different stories within the book of John:

1. **Jesus.** He is the main character in every story. John puts Jesus on display, emphasizing how Jesus came on a mission to seek and save the lost (Luke 19:10).

2. **Jesus' first disciples.** Andrew, Peter, Philip, and Nathanael were normal Jewish men. They likely weren't highly educated and were lowly fishermen, yet Jesus called them to be part of His inner circle.

3. **Nicodemus.** He was a highly educated Pharisee and devout Jew who followed the rules of Judaism very strictly. Nicodemus came to Jesus in the darkness of the night with much curiosity to meet Him and understand His teachings.

4. **The woman at the well.** She was a Samaritan woman who had five different husbands yet still could not quench the thirst of her soul. She went to the well in the midday heat alone, not realizing Jesus had a divine encounter planned for her.

5. **The man born blind.** A marginalized man who was blind since birth not only received his physical sight through Jesus' powerful miracle, but even greater than that, he received *spiritual sight* and saw Jesus for who He truly is.

6. **Lazarus, Martha, and Mary.** They were siblings who were all close friends with Jesus. Lazarus became sick and died. Martha and Mary both turned to Jesus in grief and sorrow but also in genuine faith. They wished Jesus had been there sooner to heal Lazarus, not realizing that Jesus had an even greater plan for Lazarus to come to life once again.

7. **Thomas.** One of Jesus' disciples who was filled with doubt after hearing that Jesus had risen from the grave. Thomas refused to believe that Jesus was alive until he could see and touch Jesus himself.

These next seven weeks will be filled with emotion, adventure, and deep self-reflection as you encounter Jesus in every story. Just as He was pursuing the hearts of many people in the Gospel of John, so He is continually pursuing your heart today. As you read the stories of real men and women who felt the call from Jesus in their lives to follow Him, you'll find yourself relating to their journeys of faith and their deepest emotions. Through these seven stories, Jesus will transform your heart and call you into deeper intimacy with Himself.

Overview of the EASY Bible Study Method

From Ashley, Taylor, and Ellen

As you read through the gospel of John, your guide will be the EASY Bible Study Method. This method makes studying Scripture a bit more straightforward allowing you to connect with God more deeply and personally.

If you are wondering why we call it the EASY Bible Study Method, EASY is an acronym to help you remember each step to study, process, and apply Scripture to your life. Here, we will give you a simple overview of the EASY Method, but if you want a full guide to it, check out our book, *The EASY Bible Study Method.*

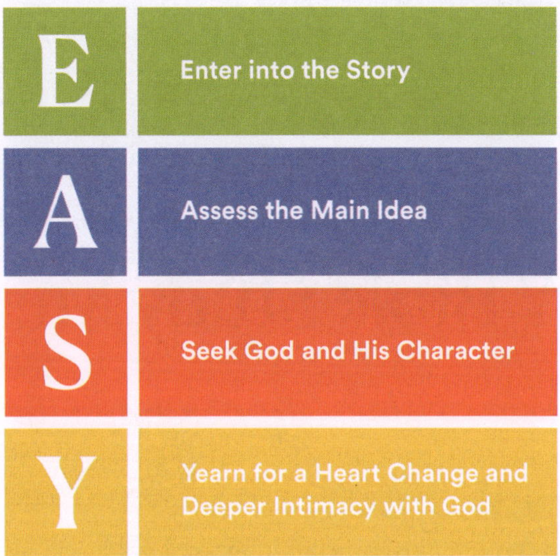

E Enter into the Story

The first step is to *Enter into the Story*. You will learn how to step into a Bible story by reading the text slowly and thoughtfully. You will also discover the importance of context when reading Scripture and how to identify the context. In essence, you will become a keen observer when reading the Bible and learn how to ask insightful questions. Here are the main steps to entering into the story that we practice throughout this study:

- Pray before reading
- Read the text slowly and thoughtfully
- Determine the context
  - Where does this fit in the storyline of the Bible?
  - Who was the original author?
  - Who was the original audience and what were they going through?
- Put yourself in the story
- Ask good questions

Assess the Main Idea

Next, you will learn how to *Assess the Main Idea* of a Scripture passage by highlighting key points and themes through annotation, paraphrasing, and uncovering the passage's meaning. We know that may sound intimidating right now, but we promise you can do it! Stick with us! And as you work through those steps, the main idea will naturally emerge. Here are the key steps to assessing the main idea that we will use throughout this study:

Annotate the passage (identifying keywords and themes)

- Highlight or circle keywords and phrases, make notes of the context of the passage, ask questions, define words, connect ideas, note God and His character

Paraphrase the passage in your own words

- Break the text into chunks, summarize each chunk into bite-size pieces, and then write one- to two-sentence paraphrases
- Ask yourself: What is the main idea of this passage?

Seek God and His Character

Third, we will show you how to *Seek God and His Character* by looking for explicit and implicit qualities and characteristics of God. Seeking these out aims to allow you to grow closer to God the Father, Son, and Holy Spirit by gaining a deeper understanding of who He is. You will realize how knowing His character shapes your thoughts about Him, feelings toward Him, and your actions. Here are the main steps to seeking God and His character that we will apply throughout this study:

Write out a list of who God is from the passage. ("God is ____________")

- Find explicit qualities and characteristics of God
  - Attributes plainly written in the text
- Find implicit qualities and characteristics of God
  - Look at the context clues, mainly actions, to find attributes not plainly found

Yearn for a Heart Change and Deeper Intimacy with God

Finally, you'll be encouraged to *Yearn for a Heart Change and Deeper Intimacy with God*. You will learn the importance of desiring Him to personally meet you where you are so you can be transformed by Him and His Word.[2] Here are the main steps to yearning for a heart change that we will practice throughout this study:

- Journal questions for inward transformation of heart and mind
- Journal questions for outward application

Dig Deeper

DIG DEEPER

Each week, we will close our study on Day 5 by digging deeper into the passage. This is where you will take your Bible study time a step further and learn important study tools, such as how to read commentaries and look into the historical and cultural context of a passage. Along with this, you will learn how to connect more deeply with a passage through prayer, journaling, art, worship, and memorization. Digging deeper is your opportunity to become like a sponge and soak up all the extra nutrients the passage has to offer. It is one of our favorite parts of Bible study!

Let's Begin!

Whether you are completely new to studying Scripture or if you are giving it another go, we are excited you have chosen to use the EASY Bible Study Method to study John with us! Let's start by opening our Bibles up to the gospel of John and going back to the very beginning.

WEEK 1

Receive or Reject

John 1:1–18

From Ashley

Have you ever felt like the rug was pulled out from under you? The first year of marriage felt a lot like that for me. After I walked down the aisle, it wasn't just my last name that changed. I packed my bags, left my childhood home and family, and stepped into a brand-new life in a brand-new town. I had to learn how to be married, make new friends while battling social anxiety, and figure out what it means to be a pastor's wife. On top of it all, I was experiencing depression and overwhelming waves of self-doubt.

My new husband patiently and lovingly walked with me through it all—he never left my side. He constantly reminded me of God's love for me and that **I am God's child: accepted, loved, and secure in Jesus**. It was that truth alone that carried me through the valley. Perhaps someone in your life has done the same for you in a difficult season.

John emphasized this same message to his readers: **Through Jesus' great love and sacrifice, we are welcomed into God's family**. In John 1:1–18, he boldly proclaimed Jesus as God. Though many rejected Jesus, the invitation to become a child of God remains open to all who believe.

WEEK 1 | DAY 1

Written So That You May Believe

Enter into the Story

To start your Bible study time, you will enter into the story. This is your opportunity to slow down and enjoy today's passage. It is full of incredible beauty and truth! There may be things you don't fully understand, and that's okay. Just keep moving forward, and you will be surprised at how much you learn by the end of this week's study.

Prayer

Start your Bible study time with this prayer. Quiet your heart, slow down, and read each word out loud to the Lord:

Dear Lord, soften my heart and open my eyes to behold wonderful things out of your Word. Amen.

Read slowly and thoughtfully

Open your Bible to John 1:1–18. Read it slowly and thoughtfully. The passage is also included for you here.

At the start of each week, we encourage you to read the passage while also listening to an audio version. Hearing and reading together can help you understand it more deeply. You can find audio readings on a Bible app or online.

Listen to the text while reading

John 1:1–18

The Word Became Flesh

1 In the beginning was the Word, and the Word was with God, and the
Word was God. **2** He was in the beginning with God. **3** All things were made
through him, and without him was not any thing made that was made.
4 In him was life, and the life was the light of men. **5** The light shines in the
darkness, and the darkness has not overcome it.

6 There was a man sent from God, whose name was John. **7** He came as a
witness, to bear witness about the light, that all might believe through him.
8 He was not the light, but came to bear witness about the light.

9 The true light, which gives light to everyone, was coming into the world.
10 He was in the world, and the world was made through him, yet the world
did not know him. **11** He came to his own, and his own people did not receive him. **12** But to all who did receive him, who believed in his name, he
gave the right to become children of God, **13** who were born, not of blood
nor of the will of the flesh nor of the will of man, but of God.

14 And the Word became flesh and dwelt among us, and we have seen
his glory, glory as of the only Son from the Father, full of grace and truth.
15 (John bore witness about him, and cried out, "This was he of whom I
said, 'He who comes after me ranks before me, because he was before me.'")
16 For from his fullness we have all received, grace upon grace. **17** For the
law was given through Moses; grace and truth came through Jesus Christ.
18 No one has ever seen God; the only God, who is at the Father's side, he has
made him known.

Write down your insights. What stands out to you initially? Also, note any questions you have while reading the text.

Context of The Gospel of John

Author

John one of Jesus' closest disciples and friends

Audience

Jews and Gentiles (non-Jewish people)

Date

Likely around AD 85–95. Believers were facing persecution and the early church was growing

Location

John likely wrote to believers living in Asia Minor near Ephesus (modern-day Turkey)

Purpose

". . . but these are written **so that you may believe that Jesus is the Christ, the Son of God,** and that by believing you may have life in his name." (John 20:31 ESV)

Determine Context

You may be wondering **who the author, John, is**. Most credible sources will tell you that he was one of Jesus' closest disciples. He is not to be confused with John the Baptist, whom you read about in John 1:6–7 and appears again in John 1:19–34. Although the author John never directly mentions his name, he refers to himself as the disciple "whom Jesus loved" multiple times throughout the book (John 13:23; 20:2; 21:7, 20).

John walked with Jesus throughout His earthly ministry. He is considered to be one of **Jesus' closest friends**. John was there when Jesus died on the cross, saw Jesus alive after He rose from the grave, and watched Jesus ascend into heaven. It is absolutely incredible that we have a firsthand witness account of the life of Jesus through His beloved disciple, John.

John originally wrote this story to **Jews and Gentiles** (*Gentile* means a non-Jew), **encouraging them to believe in Jesus as the Messiah and Son of God**.

Look up John 20:31. It explains why John wrote this book. Write down the verse here:

The word ***belief* is used nearly 100 times** within the book of John. It's a theme within John's gospel that we cannot escape. Every story and moment that John captured is included to help lead his readers to believe in Jesus.

Reflect

As you start this journey through John, reflect on where your heart is now. Circle where you currently stand on this belief spectrum, and honestly journal where you are in your walk with Jesus.

Do you believe in Jesus as your Lord and Savior?

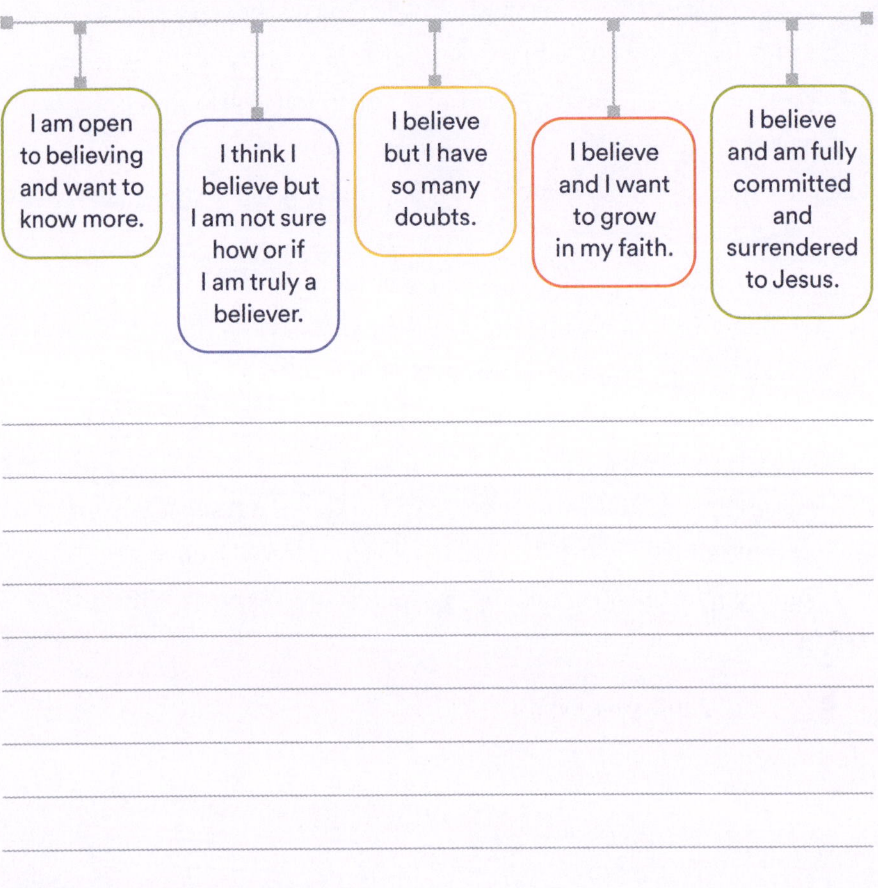

WEEK 1 | DAY 2

It All Starts Here

Assess the Main Idea

Now that we have become familiar with John 1:1–18, our goal is to assess the main idea and figure out what this passage means.

Annotate

Reread John 1:1–18, but this time focus on some key components of the passage (if you'd like, revisit the passage from Day 1 and do your annotations there):

Highlight the name **Jesus** and the other **names of Jesus** in purple:

- The Word, the only Son, Jesus Christ, God the only Son

Highlight the following **character references** in green:

- **John the Baptist.** He was Jesus' relative (Luke 1:36), whom God called to pave the way for Jesus. His ministry was all about **pointing people to Jesus**; that's why the text says John "bore witness about him" (John 1:15). John the Baptist is not to be confused with the author John, who was Jesus' disciple.

Identify **themes**:

- Circle **life** and **light** in purple
- Circle the **world** in red
- Circle **grace** and **truth** in blue
- Highlight any forms of **belief** in yellow:
  - believe, believed

Ashley's Annotation Example: **John 1:1–18**

Jesus Jesus

1 In the beginning was the Word, and the Word was with God,
and the Word was God. **2** He was in the beginning with God.
3 All things were made through him, and without him was not
any thing made that was made. **4** In him was life, and the life
was the light of men. **5** The light shines in the darkness, and the
darkness has not overcome it.

John wanted to show that Jesus is the ultimate communication of God to humans. Jesus is God and reveals who God is.

Life: Jesus is life (John 14:6). True life can only be found in Him.

Light: Jesus reveals truth and overcomes spiritual darkness.

6 There was a man sent from God, whose name was John. **7** He
came as a witness, to bear witness about the light, that all might
believe through him. **8** He was not the light, but came to bear
witness about the light.

John the Baptist pointed people to Jesus.

9 The true light, which gives light to everyone, was coming into
the world. **10** He was in the world, and the world was made
through him, yet the world did not know him. **11** He came to his
own, and his own people did not receive him. **12** But to all who
did receive him, who believed in his name, he gave the right to
become children of God, **13** who were born, not of blood nor of
the will of the flesh nor of the will of man, but of God.

World: full of sin, brokenness, and in rebellion against God. This is the world God so loves (John 3:16).

14 And the Word became flesh and dwelt among us, and we
have seen his glory, glory as of the only Son from the Father,

full of grace and truth. **15** (John bore witness about him, and
cried out, "This was he of whom I said, 'He who comes after me
ranks before me, because he was before me.'") **16** For from his
fullness we have all received, grace upon grace. **17** For the law
was given through Moses; grace and truth came through Jesus
Christ. **18** No one has ever seen God; God the only Son, who is
at the Father's side, he has made him known.

Truth: There is nothing wrong or false within Jesus. He embodies truth. He is the truth (John 14:6). He perfectly reflects and reveals God.

Grace: Unmerited grace and favor. Forgiveness, salvation, and a restored relationship with God through Jesus.

Main Idea

As you look back on your annotations, what color is repeated the most throughout the passage?

Yep—**it's purple!** We highlighted the character qualities of Jesus in purple and circled light and life in purple, too. It's quite obvious that Jesus is the main idea of this passage and the central theme of John's opening introduction to his book.

John intentionally wrote this prologue *to lay the foundation* for everything else that is to come. Not only did he want to introduce us to Jesus, but to immediately show us **who Jesus is** and **what His incredible mission is.**

Look back in the passage and write down:

Who is Jesus?

What is Jesus' mission?

Paraphrase

John 1:1–18 is split into four sections for paraphrasing. Writing the passage in your own words will help you **grasp the main idea of this passage**. I started by paraphrasing John 1:1–5 and John 1:6–8 for you. You can finish the rest. Make sure to keep these short, between one to two sentences. Look back at John 1:1–18 to help you paraphrase.

John 1:1–5:

We are introduced to the Word, who is Jesus. He was with God in the beginning. He is God, and through Him, God made all things. In Him is light and life.

John 1:6–8:

We are introduced to John the Baptist. He is Jesus' witness so that all would believe in Jesus.

John 1:9–13:

John 1:14–18:

Reflect

Today, we have learned that Jesus came into the world, revealing God's glory and grace. John bore witness to Jesus, and although many rejected Jesus, anyone who believed became a child of God. Close today's study by writing down one new thing you learned about God.

WEEK 1 | DAY 3

Author of Existence

Seek God and His Character

Now, it's time to dive deep into who God is. John filled these first eighteen verses with incredible insights into God's character. As you read through Scripture, God will reveal Himself to you as Father, Son (Jesus), and Holy Spirit. Each person of the Trinity is fully God, yet also has unique roles and characteristics. In John's book, we will learn a lot about who Jesus is specifically.

The Trinity means one God in three persons—Father, Son, and Holy Spirit—who have always existed in a loving relationship.

Implicit

- Is not directly stated
- Requires a level of discernment
- Is found through context clues
    - Look to see what can be implied about God through actions, etc.

Explicit

- Is directly stated, no interpretation required
- Does not require discernment to know

When studying God in a passage, there is explicit (plainly stated) and implicit (contextually implied) information about God. Today, we will look at one of Jesus' **implicit** attributes from John 1.

Jesus is the Creator

Implicit Characteristics of God

Read John 1:1–5. John starts his gospel with a big statement: In the beginning was Jesus, and through Him all things were created (John 1:1–3). An **implicit** attribute of Jesus from this text is that *Jesus is the Creator.*

Let's take a closer look at this:

Genesis 1:1 says, "In the beginning, God . . ."
John 1:1 says, "In the beginning was the Word . . ."

It is no coincidence that Genesis and John both start with "In the beginning . . ." John is echoing the creation story and taking us back to the very beginning of time.

God spoke creation into existence with **His words** (Gen. 1:3). Now John is telling us that Jesus is **the Word** and "all things were made through him, and without him was not any thing made that was made" (John 1:3).

Look up Colossians 1:15–16 in the English Standard Version (ESV). Fill in the blanks here:

> Jesus "is the ____________ of the invisible God, the firstborn of all creation. For by him all things were ______________, in heaven and on earth, visible and invisible, whether thrones or dominions or rulers or authorities—all things were ______________ through him and for him."

But why should it matter to you and me that Jesus is the Creator? Here are three reasons:

1. It shows that Jesus is more than just a good man who walked the earth thousands of years ago. He is the author of existence. **He is divine. He is all-powerful. He is God.**
2. It should lead us to trust in Him. Jesus "upholds the universe by the

word of his power" (Heb. 1:3). He controls and sustains everything He created, including the smallest details of our lives. If He holds everything together (Col. 1:17), **we can also trust Him to hold us together**.

3. Jesus created the world to be a perfect place, but sin entered in and ruined God's original design. Yet that is not the end of the story—Jesus created the world and will one day redeem and restore it. We all know that this world is not our home. We long for a new creation, a world without suffering, pain, and sin. **Jesus said He would make all things new** (Rev. 21:5). He will re-create the world into a new creation.

Meditate

Write out John 1:1–5. Then, repeat it out loud twice. Close your time by praising Jesus for being your Creator, Life, and Light.

WEEK 1 | DAY 4

Enfolded into God's Family

Yearn for a Heart Change and Deeper Intimacy with God

Today, you will reflect on and apply John 1:1–18 to your life.

The **ultimate goal of a Bible study** is to meet with Jesus personally, grow your connection with Him, and be transformed by God's Word.

Read

Read again John 1:1–18 and focus on the theme of **receiving** Jesus.

The passage says that Jesus came into the world that He created, yet was **rejected** by His own people (vv. 9–11). Although many people chose not to **receive** Him, those "who did **receive** him, who believed in his name, he gave the right to become children of God" (v. 12, emphasis added).

Throughout John's gospel, we meet many people who faced this question: **Will you reject or receive Jesus?** Although many people received Jesus, sadly, more rejected Him.

Even though Jesus knew He would be rejected, He still came. He still extended His heart to His people and the Gentiles, and He is extending His heart to you and me today.

Reflect

Jesus endured the deepest pain imaginable so that you could be welcomed into His family. How does it make you feel to know that Jesus came to this earth and willingly faced rejection—all because of His incredible love for you?

Cross-reference

John points out that those who choose to receive Jesus become His children. The theme of adoption and acceptance into God's family is a common theme throughout the New Testament. Look up **Romans 8:15–17** and write down *what you learn about being God's child.*

Now read this devotional reading inspired from **Romans 8:15–17.** Highlight or underline what you learn about being God's child.

> And you did not receive the "spirit of religious duty," leading you back into the fear of never being good enough. But you have received the "Spirit of full acceptance," enfolding you into the family of God. And you will never feel orphaned, for as he rises up within us, our spirits join him in saying the words of tender affection, "Beloved Father!"
>
> For the Holy Spirit makes God's fatherhood real to us as he whispers into our innermost being, "You are God's beloved child!"

> So you have not received a spirit that makes you fearful slaves. Instead, you received God's Spirit when he adopted you as his own children. Now we call him, "Abba, Father." For his Spirit joins with our spirit to affirm that we are God's children. And since we are his children, we are his heirs. In fact, together with Christ we are heirs of God's glory. But if we are to share his glory, we must also share his suffering. (Rom. 8:15–17 NLT)

Being God's child means that we have been enfolded into God's family. We are no longer orphans. We have a home, a family, and a good, good Father. Jesus has opened the door for us to have an intimate relationship with Himself and God the Father through the Holy Spirit, who lives within us. It is because of God's great love for us that we belong to Him (1 John 3:1). At our core, this is who we are: children of God.

But being His child doesn't mean that life will be easy. Rather, it means that we are joined to Christ in His glory *and* suffering. One day, we will be glorified with Christ. Our bodies will be made new, sin will be no more, and we will live for all eternity in God's love. But for now, we journey through trials and sufferings, taking up our cross daily— just as Jesus did—because we are joined to Him. (We will learn more about this next week.)

Prayer

As you finish today's study, spend a moment reading through this list of why it's significant to be God's child. Choose one that stands out to you and look up the verse. Close your time praying, connecting to God as your Father, and thanking Him for adopting you into His family.

Being God's Child means . . .

- I am loved by a good Father – John 3:1
- I am forgiven – Ephesians 1:7
- I am chosen and adopted – Romans 8:15
- I am an heir of God – Romans 8:17
- I am a new person – 2 Corinthians 5:17
- I am forever in Jesus' hands – John 10:28
- I am called to be like God – Ephesians 5:1
- I am God's workmanship – Ephesians 2:10
- I have hope in Christ forever – 1 Peter 1:3
- I am never alone – John 14:18
- I am secure – Psalm 94:14
- I have God's Spirit within me – Romans 8:14

WEEK 1 | DAY 5

Believe Is a Verb

Dig Deeper

DIG DEEPER

Over the past few days, we have learned a lot about who Jesus is. Today, we will dig even deeper by looking at what a commentary has to say about John 1:10–12. Reading commentaries can help grow your understanding of the text and answer your questions.

Read

The commentary we will look at today is *John: Verse by Verse* by Dr. Grant Osborne. Before reading through the excerpts that I've included from this commentary, **read John 1:10–12.**

Commentary

As you read through the following two paragraphs from *John: Verse by Verse*, focus on the main theme we have been learning about—**rejecting versus receiving Jesus**. Highlight anything that stands out to you from this scholar's perspective of the text.

What's a Commentary?

A scholar's (or multiple scholars') explanation and interpretation of the biblical text including historical, cultural, and theological background to help the reader better understand the text.

Rejecting Jesus

Commentary

The Word entered this world in order to experience **rejection** and to die in order to save it. . . . It would be expected that the world of humankind would love and worship the very one who had created them and their world (v. 3) and who had loved them enough to become one of them. Instead, they failed to recognize him. The verb behind "recognize" (ginōskō) doesn't just mean they failed to know who he was but rather that **they rejected who he was**. To "know" him would demand repentance and conversion, a complete change of perspective on life. They were unwilling to take that step. They demanded Christ meet them on their own terms, and so were **unwilling to accept** the revealed Word and the salvation-offering Savior.[3]

Wow! Dr. Osborne packed a lot into those thoughts on rejecting Jesus. Don't worry if you didn't catch it all. We will go back through it and unpack it.

Let's talk about what it means to **reject** Jesus according to *John: Verse by Verse*:

1. Jesus knew more than a thing or two about rejection. In love, He came to earth to save His very own creation, yet experienced the cruelest possible rejection ever known to man. "He was despised and rejected by men, a man of sorrows and acquainted with grief" (Isa. 53:3).

Jesus Rejected

Jesus was betrayed, abandoned, falsely accused, beaten, mocked, flogged, scorned,shamed, and nailed to a cross to suffer a brutal death.
For further study: Isaiah 53

2. The world didn't just fail to acknowledge Jesus; they fully rejected Him and His way.

3. They were unwilling to accept Jesus because that required **repentance**. Repentance is a wholehearted turning away from sin and a sincere turning toward God in devotion and obedience.

Reflect

Jeffrey Meyers writes, "In the life of the follower of Jesus, there is no standing still. We are always walking in the Christian life either away from or toward our destination as mature sons and daughters of God."[4] Is there any area of your life where you are currently walking away from God and His way? Use the space below to share honestly with God your struggles. **Wholeheartedly repent and turn back to Him.**

Now, focus on **receiving Jesus**. Highlight anything that stands out to you from this scholar's perspective of the text.

Receiving Jesus

> John divides the world into two groups—**those who reject and those who accept**. In verse 12 God gives those who accept and believe a new status and authority... **Receiving** and believing are the antithesis of "not knowing/receiving" and are virtual synonyms, with "believe" another key term in John. . . It is always a verb, stressing **the dynamic process of faith-decision**. This belief is "in his name," meaning the full reality and person behind "the Word." **To believe is to immerse one's self in all that is Jesus as the Word of God . . .** To "give the right" means for the Word to bestow "authority"... on the believers as "children of God." They have the right to belong to a new family, and their status changes from peasant to prince. The new birth makes them part of the royal household of heaven.[5]

Let's unpack this a bit more!

1. Those who believe have a new identity: children of God! We are part of God's family and enter into His Kingdom of Light.

2. Receiving and believing in Jesus is the opposite of not knowing Jesus and rejecting Him.

3. Believe is a verb. It's about actively putting our faith and trust in Jesus and following after Him. It's about repenting from our old way of life and turning to Him.

Colossians 1:13–14

"For he has rescued us
from the dominion
of darkness
and brought us into
the kingdom of the Son
he loves, in whom we
have redemption,
the forgiveness of sins."

Reflect

Believing in Jesus means immersing yourself in all that Jesus is, as the Word of God.[6] Yet, this may look different on our good days and our bad days. Give a specific example of what it looks like to actively believe in Jesus in your daily life when things are going well. What about when you're walking through a valley? How do you put your faith and trust in Him when life is hard?

The Journey Continues

This week, we learned that Jesus was more than simply a man who walked on the earth thousands of years ago. While He is fully human, He is also fully God. He is the Creator of the universe. He is the Light of the World. He is true Life. He is the direct communication of God the Father, revealing who God is. And He has opened His heart to the world so that anyone who believes in Him can become God's child.

As we continue our study next week, we will examine the lives of a few normal guys whom Jesus called to leave everything to follow Him. Did they receive or reject Jesus? Let's find out!

Discussion Questions

To help you reflect on the week of study, here are optional discussion questions that you can discuss with a friend, mentor, or small group.

1. Where are you currently in your walk with Jesus? Be honest and explain, if you can, why you are in that place. Share your desire for where you would like to be.
2. What did you learn about John the Baptist's mission this week? To discover more about it, read Matthew 11:7–11. What are a few ways you can humble yourself, point others to Christ, and become the least in God's Kingdom?
3. What does the author John make clear about Jesus within the first eighteen verses of the book of John? In other words, **who is Jesus** in this key passage?
4. How does John take the reader back to the creation of the world? What significance does this have to who Jesus is? Why should this matter to you?
5. We learned that repentance is a wholehearted turning away from sin and a sincere turning toward God in devotion and obedience. What is the Holy Spirit nudging you to turn away from? What action steps will you take to turn back to Christ and His way?

WEEK 2

Come and Follow

John 1:35–51

By Ashley

I had a huge moment of clarity during my teenage years that changed my life forever. Let me explain.

I grew up in a Christian home and knew Jesus loved me from a young age. But there's a big difference between head knowledge and heart knowledge. Just because I understood it intellectually didn't mean it had impacted my emotions, beliefs, and actions.

Everything changed, though, when I connected with a group of friends who passionately loved Jesus. The way they lived for Him—not just in words, but in every part of their lives—captivated me.

These friends weren't cultural Christians. They were disciples. A disciple doesn't just wear the name "Christian"—they follow Jesus fully, leaving behind what society teaches to live for God's Kingdom.

In John 1:35–51, we meet Jesus' first disciples. They were just ordinary guys. But Jesus saw them and called them to follow Him in His mission to seek and save the lost. They left their old lives and walked closely with Him.

And friend, as you'll see this week, Jesus is calling us too—to leave our old lives behind, grow in our devotion, and join Him in spreading His name to the world.

WEEK 2 | DAY 1

The Cost of Discipleship

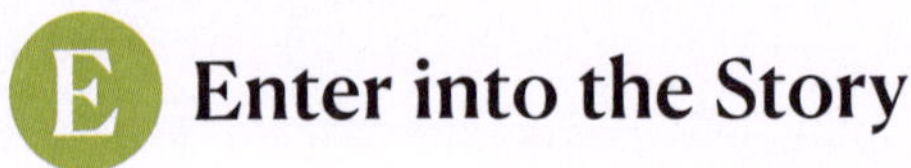

Enter into the Story

Prayer

Start your Bible study time with this prayer. Quiet your heart, slow down, and read each word out loud to the Lord:

Dear Lord, just as the first disciples boldly followed You, make my heart sensitive to receive Your call over my life to follow You too. Amen.

Read slowly and thoughtfully

Open your Bible to John 1:35–51. Read it slowly and thoughtfully. The passage is also included for you here.

Listen to the text while reading

John 1:35–51

Jesus Calls the First Disciples

35 The next day again John was standing with two of his disciples, **36** and he looked at Jesus as he walked by and said, “Behold, the Lamb of God!” **37** The two disciples heard him say this, and they followed Jesus. **38** Jesus turned and saw them following and said to them, “What are you seeking?” And they said to him, “Rabbi” (which means Teacher), “where are you staying?” **39** He said to them, “Come and you will see.” So they came and saw where he was staying, and they stayed with him that day, for it was about the tenth hour. **40** One of the two who heard John speak and followed Jesus was Andrew, Simon Peter’s brother. **41** He first found his own brother Simon and said to him, “We have found the Messiah” (which means Christ). **42** He brought him to Jesus. Jesus looked at him and said, “You are Simon the son of John. You shall be called Cephas” (which means Peter).

Jesus Calls Philip and Nathanael

43 The next day Jesus decided to go to Galilee. He found Philip and said to him, “Follow me.” **44** Now Philip was from Bethsaida, the city of Andrew and Peter. **45** Philip found Nathanael and said to him, “We have found him of whom Moses in the Law and also the prophets wrote, Jesus of Nazareth, the son of Joseph.” **46** Nathanael said to him, “Can anything good come out of Nazareth?” Philip said to him, “Come and see.” **47** Jesus saw Nathanael coming toward him and said of him, “Behold, an Israelite indeed, in whom there is no deceit!” **48** Nathanael said to him, “How do you know me?” Jesus answered him, “Before Philip called you, when you were under the fig tree, I saw you.” **49** Nathanael answered him, “Rabbi, you are the Son of God! You are the King of Israel!” **50** Jesus answered him, “Because I said to you, ‘I saw you under the fig tree,’ do you believe? You will see greater things than these.” **51** And he said to him, “Truly, truly, I say to you, you will see heaven opened, and the angels of God ascending and descending on the Son of Man.”

Write down your insights. What stands out to you initially? Also, note any questions you have while reading the text.

This passage introduces us to the first disciples Jesus called: Andrew, Peter, Philip, Nathanael, and a disciple who is not named. Each of these men came to Jesus and believed in Him.

Let's look at what it means to be a disciple.

Disciple	A disciple is simply a **follower** or **student** of a teacher. They learn from their teacher, believe in their teachings, and try to live like them.

Jesus asked His disciples not only to believe in His teachings but also to believe *in Him and leave everything to follow Him*. They left their jobs, families, and comfort to follow Him. They were confident that He was more than just a man. They saw something unique in Jesus and risked it all to follow Him.

Look up these verses and respond to these questions to learn more about **what was expected of Jesus' disciples**:

1. According to **Luke 5:27–28**, what did Jesus' disciples, such as Levi, leave behind?

2. In **Matthew 10:37**, Jesus instructs His disciples to love Him and place Him above what?

3. Read **Matthew 16:24**. How did Jesus tell His disciples to deny themselves?

4. In **Matthew 19:16–22**, Jesus tells a rich man to give up what to follow Him? Was this man willing to give it up?

Jesus asked His disciples to leave behind everything, including family, comfort, and financial security. But He didn't instruct them to lose it all and gain nothing in return. The reward Jesus offered was far greater than what they would give up. They gained Jesus Himself and eternal life through Him (Matt. 19:29).

Reflect

Like those early disciples, following Jesus requires that you put Him first in your life. He needs to take priority over your family, friends, romantic interests, dreams, career aspirations, finances, comfort, and anything else that seeks to hold your attention and affection over Him. What might be keeping you distracted from deepening your relationship with Jesus and following Him wherever He may take you?

Put yourself in the story

Read John 1:35–39. If I were to put myself in the shoes of the first disciples, I would have felt honored, welcomed, and deeply loved to have been chosen to spend more time with Jesus. Receiving such an intimate invitation would have made me feel special and seen.

The disciples likely stayed with Jesus for hours, sharing food, conversation, laughs, and a deep connection. Oh, how I long to have been invited to this intimate gathering! I'm sure the disciples realized Jesus was like no other man they had ever met.

Now, put yourself in the disciples' shoes. Close your time journaling about how you would feel if Jesus had invited you to see where He was staying and spend time with Him.

WEEK 2 | DAY 2

Meeting the Messiah

Assess the Main Idea

Now that we have become familiar with John 1:35–51, our goal is to assess the main idea and figure out what this passage means.

Annotate

Reread John 1:35–51, but this time focus on some key components of the passage, such as:

Highlight the name **Jesus** and the other **names of Jesus** in purple:

- The Lamb of God, Rabbi (Teacher), Messiah, Christ, Jesus of Nazareth, Son of God, King of Israel, Son of Man

Highlight the following **character references** in green:

- Andrew, Simon Peter, Philip, and Nathanael

Identify **themes:**

- Circle **come** in red
- Circle **follow** in blue
- Highlight any forms of **belief** in yellow:
    - believe, believed

Ashley's Annotation Example: **John 1:35–51**

35 The next day again John was standing with two of his disciples, **36** and he
looked at Jesus as he walked by and said, "Behold, the Lamb of God!" **37** The
Name of Jesus: Lamb of God
two disciples heard him say this, and they followed Jesus.

38 Jesus turned and saw them following and said to them, "What are you
seeking?" And they said to him, "Rabbi" (which means Teacher), "where are you
Name of Jesus: Rabbi: Teacher
staying?" **39** He said to them, "Come and you will see." So they came and saw where
he was staying, and they stayed with him that day, for it was about the tenth hour.

40 One of the two who heard John speak and followed Jesus was Andrew,
Simon Peter's brother. **41** He first found his own brother Simon and said to him,
"We have found the Messiah" (which means Christ). **42** He brought him to Jesus.
Name of Jesus: Messiah: Christ
Jesus looked at him and said, "You are Simon the son of John. You shall be called
Cephas" (which means Peter).

Jesus Calls Philip and Nathanael

43 The next day Jesus decided to go to Galilee. He found Philip and said to him,
"Follow me." **44** Now Philip was from Bethsaida, the city of Andrew and Peter.

45 Philip found Nathanael and said to him, "We have found him of whom Moses
in the Law and also the prophets wrote, Jesus of Nazareth, the son of Joseph."
Name of Jesus: Jesus of Nazareth, the son of Joseph
46 Nathanael said to him, "Can anything good come out of Nazareth?" Philip said
to him, "Come and see."

47 Jesus saw Nathanael coming toward him and said of him, “Behold, an
Israelite indeed, in whom there is no deceit!” **48** Nathanael said to him, “How
do you know me?” Jesus answered him, “Before Philip called you, when you
were under the fig tree, I saw you.” **49** Nathanael answered him, “Rabbi, you are
the Son of God! You are the King of Israel!”
Name of Jesus: Son of God *Name of Jesus: King of Israel*
50 Jesus answered him, “Because I said to you, ‘I saw you under the fig tree,’ do
you believe? You will see greater things than these.” **51** And he said to him, “Truly,
truly, I say to you, you will see heaven opened, and the angels of God ascending
and descending on the Son of Man.”
Name of Jesus: Son of Man

Paraphrase

How did each of the disciples first meet Jesus? Let’s summarize each one’s story in one to two sentences. I’ll start with Andrew, and then you can complete Simon Peter, Philip, and Nathanael. Use John 1:35–51 to help you.

Andrew:

He was a disciple of John the Baptist first, then follows Jesus after hearing John point to Jesus as “The Lamb of God!” He also introduces his brother to Jesus.

Simon Peter:

Philip:

Nathaniel:

The disciples each came to Jesus in a different way. Some followed Jesus right away, while others were curious yet skeptical. They each saw something unique within Jesus and opened their hearts to **come** to Him and start **following** Him.

Main Idea

Concluding all that we have learned so far, what do you think **the main point of John's message is in John 1:35–51**?

Reflect

How does this passage help grow and deepen your faith in Jesus?

Do you think you are more like **Andrew**, who was "all-in" and followed Jesus right away? Or are you more like **Nathanael**, who was a bit skeptical about who Jesus was at first? Explain why you are more of an Andrew or a Nathanael.

Just as Andrew and Philip introduced others to Jesus, whom do you have on your heart to introduce to Jesus? What are some practical steps you can take this week to share Jesus with this person? Develop a plan and write it here.

WEEK 2 | DAY 3

Discovering Seven Names of Jesus

Seek God and His Character

There are so many different characteristics of Jesus. Throughout John, we will discover new pieces of the "Jesus puzzle" that we will continue to put together. This week's passage has seven unique **puzzle pieces** or names that convey explicit characteristics of Jesus. Yesterday, you highlighted these names in purple.

Implicit Characteristics of God

Reread John 1:35–51 and write out the seven names of Jesus mentioned in it. To further your understanding, read the added commentary about each name of Jesus.

Jesus is the L ________________________ **(John 1:36)**

- Lambs were used for sacrifice in the Old Testament to take away sin. Jesus is our ultimate and final sacrifice, dying for our sins (Isa. 53:7).

Jesus is the R ________________________ **(John 1:38)**

- *Rabbi* means teacher. Usually, rabbis taught the law and had students or disciples who followed them closely.

Jesus is the M__________________________ (John 1:41)

- *Messiah* which means "Christ" in Greek and "Anointed One" in Hebrew. Jesus is the Savior of the world, the long-awaited Jewish Anointed One that the Israelites were waiting for.

Jesus of N__________________________ (John 1:45)

- Jesus grew up in the town of Nazareth in Galilee. Nazareth was an insignificant and humble town with nothing special about it.

Jesus is the S__________________________ (John 1:49)

- Jesus was conceived by the Holy Spirit (Luke 1:35), has a special relationship with God the Father (Matt. 3:17), and was given by God to die for our sins (John 3:16).

Jesus is the K__________________________ (John 1:49)

- Jesus fulfills Old Testament prophecies, where God promised a king through David's line to rule forever (2 Sam. 7:12–16). The Jewish people wanted a political king to overthrow the Romans, but Jesus came as a spiritual king to save the world from sin and death.

Jesus is the S__________________________ (John 1:51)

- This title focuses on Jesus' humanity and shows that Jesus was fully human (Dan. 7:13–14).

Jesus is the Lamb of God, Teacher, Anointed Savior, and King, who is fully human and fully God. He grew up in a humble town, invited lowly fishermen into His life to be His first followers, and came to serve and give up His life (Matt. 20:28).

Just as He told Nathanael, "I saw you" (John 1:48), He also tells you, "I see you." He sees you in your pain, in your suffering, in your doubts, in your questions, in your longings, and in your fears. He sees you. He loves you. **He is the**

God of the universe, yet He knows you personally and intimately.

Just as He came for His first disciples and called them to enter His life, He calls you too—not just to say you're a Christian, but to truly know Him as a close friend and surrender your life to follow Him.

Which of these names of Jesus most intrigued you? Reflect on why this name interests you and how you may have experienced this characteristic of Jesus in your life.

Jesus is ______________________________

7 Names of Jesus in John 1:35–51

Jesus is The Son of Man

Jesus is Rabbi

Jesus is The Lamb of God

Jesus is The Messiah

Jesus of Nazareth

Jesus is The Son of God

Jesus is King of Israel

WEEK 2 | DAY 4

Come In and Stay Awhile

Yearn for a Heart Change and Deeper Intimacy with God

Today, you will reflect on and apply John 1:35–51 to your life.

Read

Reread John 1:35–51, focusing on Jesus' invitation to *come and follow*.

Jesus then asked them:

"What are you seeking?"

Jesus always asked questions aimed at people's hearts. He already knew the answers, but He was helping them process the *why* behind their actions. In the gospel of John, He also asked "whom" people sought multiple times (John 18:4, 7; 20:15). Dr. Osborne explains, "In a real sense, he is demanding, '**What do you want out of life?**'"[7]

Ultimately, the disciples were seeking Jesus as their teacher. They wanted to learn from Him and know Him on a deeper level. They asked to see where He was staying, and Jesus said:

"Come and you will see."

I love the heart of Jesus. Just like He did with these first followers, He also invites us in. We see in His interaction with Nathanael that He isn't afraid of our doubts or questions. He opens Himself to us. He asks us to come and see who He is and what He is all about. The more time we spend with Him, the more we realize we cannot live without Him.

Jesus is God and King, yet He is also a gentle and humble friend. Jesus sees you and is directly inviting you to **come and follow Him**.

Reflect

What do you want out of life? Has seeking Jesus been a priority or have you been pursuing other things above Him, such as financial security, relational happiness, academic or career success, or popularity and a loyal following? How can you rearrange your priorities and put Him first?

If you have responded to Jesus' call to follow Him, how has your life changed because of it? What have you had to give up to be His disciple?

Journal about a time you connected with Jesus in a deep and personal way. How did you know He was with you? What were you doing (or ceased doing) when you experienced His presence and felt Him near?

WEEK 2 | DAY 5

Behold the Lamb

Dig Deeper

DIG DEEPER

One of the names of Jesus we studied earlier this week was the Lamb of God. Today, we will explore the historical and cultural significance of this name. Although its importance would have been evident to the original readers of John, it requires more study for us to grasp fully.

Read John 1:29 and John 1:35–37 and focus on where the Lamb of God is mentioned.

John the Baptist helped prepare his disciples' hearts to receive Jesus. In verse 29, he calls Jesus "**the Lamb of God, who takes away the sin of the world**." Then, in verse 36, he emphasizes again that **Jesus is the Lamb of God**.

When his disciples saw Jesus walk by and heard John declare He was the Lamb of God, they couldn't help but **follow**.

Historical Cultural Context

In that culture and time period, it must have been *astoundingly rare* to hear a human being called a "lamb" who "takes away sin." Let's look into the history of this.

First, let's discuss the seriousness of sin. Sin is anything we think, say, or do that goes against God and His ways. All humans are sinful at conception (Ps. 51:5) and we have no way within ourselves to overcome our sinful nature. The consequence for sin is death (Rom. 6:23) and separation from God, who is our only source of true, eternal life.

That leads us to our second point: How do we deal with this sin? In the Old Testament, priests had the responsibility of atoning for the people's sins through animal sacrifices, which included the offering of one-year-old, unblemished lambs. However, this sacrificial system in the Old Testament was temporary. The lambs couldn't permanently take away the people's sins (Heb. 10:4). These sacrifices had to be repeated and, ultimately, served as a symbol of the seriousness of sin. These lambs pointed ahead to a greater Lamb that would one day take away the sins of the world (John 1:29).

ATONEMENT

Animals became substitutes (took the place) for the people of Israel. Although the people deserved death, an animal died in their place. This is called atonement when someone or something covers over someone's death.

If these first disciples knew the Scriptures well, they may have thought of **Isaiah 53** when John called Jesus the Lamb of God. Isaiah 53 was written by the prophet Isaiah approximately 500–700 years before Jesus' birth. Isaiah 53, in the Old Testament, is about the promised suffering servant who would one day come to suffer for Israel and ultimately die for the sins of others. This passage specifically points to the Messiah as "a lamb that is led to the slaughter" (Isa. 53:7) and "bore the sin of many" (Isa. 53:12).

Cross-reference

Read each section of Isaiah 53:3–10, then **look up and write down the provided Scripture** cross-references that show how Jesus fulfilled each of the prophecies.

Isaiah 53	*Fulfillment*
3 He was despised and rejected by men, a man of sorrows and acquainted with grief; and as one from whom men hide their faces he was despised, and we esteemed him not.	***Rejected by People – John 1:11***

Isaiah 53	***Fulfillment***
4 Surely he has borne our griefs and carried our sorrows; yet we esteemed him stricken, smitten by God, and afflicted. **5** But he was pierced for our transgressions; he was crushed for our iniquities; upon him was the chastisement that brought us peace, and with his wounds we are healed. **6** All we like sheep have gone astray; we have turned—every one—to his own way; and the Lord has laid on him the iniquity of us all.	***Bore our Sins – 1 Peter 2:22–25***
7 He was oppressed, and he was afflicted, yet he opened not his mouth; like a lamb that is led to the slaughter, and like a sheep that before its shearers is silent, so he opened not his mouth. **8** By oppression and judgment he was taken away; and as for his generation, who considered that he was cut off out of the land of the living, stricken for the transgression of my people?	***Silent Before His Accusers – Matthew 27:12***
9 And they made his grave with the wicked and with a rich man in his death, although he had done no violence, and there was no deceit in his mouth.	***Rich Man's Grave – Matthew 27:57, 59–60***

10 Yet it was the will of the Lord to crush him; he has put him to grief; when his soul makes an offering for guilt, he shall see his offspring; he shall prolong his days; the will of the Lord shall prosper in his hand.	***Jesus' Death Was God's Will – Acts 2:23***

Can you see why John's disciples were intrigued by Jesus? For hundreds of years, the Jews had been waiting for their Messiah to come. And now, here He was, right before their eyes—the Lamb of God—so **they followed Him**.

Reflect

How does understanding the historical and cultural significance of Jesus' name, the Lamb of God, help you know more about who Jesus is and better understand His mission to save the lost?

Like Jesus' disciples, what intrigues you about Jesus being the Lamb of God? And what stands out to you in Isaiah 53, knowing it was written hundreds of years before Jesus came?

The Journey Continues

Over the past two weeks, our study of John has revealed aspects of who Jesus is. We discovered that He is fully human while also being fully God. We also learned that Jesus came to earth with the purpose that anyone who believes in His name can become children of God (John 1:12).

We were given a peek into Jesus' first encounter with His disciples, who came to Him with curiosity and faith. As Jesus revealed more of Himself to them, they started to see who Jesus truly is—the Messiah the Jews had been longing and waiting for. As they spent time with Him, Jesus stirred their hearts to believe. And, as we read about these encounters, Jesus challenges us to see who He truly is and also choose to put our hope in Him.

Next week, we will focus on Jesus' encounter with Nicodemus, a very religious man. Jesus shared with Nicodemus how to be born again and receive eternal life, which challenged Nicodemus' intellectual knowledge and raises the question: Did Nicodemus put his faith in Jesus?

Discussion Questions

To help you reflect on the week of study, here are optional discussion questions that you can discuss with a friend, mentor, or small group.

1. Obeying the call to be one of Jesus' disciples is not easy. It requires prioritizing Jesus over ourselves, other relationships, and our possessions. Look up these verses and discuss what they tell us about sacrificing for the sake of following Jesus:

- Luke 14:26–27

- Luke 9:23–24

- Luke 14:33

2. We learned that Jesus is the Lamb of God, Teacher, Anointed Savior, and King who is fully human and fully God. What stands out to you the most about who Jesus is? Why?

3. Just as Andrew and Philip introduced others to Jesus, is there someone you would like to introduce to Jesus? What is holding you back from sharing Jesus with them?

4. Jesus asked His disciples a very important question: "What are you seeking?" (John 1:38). How would you answer this question? What do you want out of life?

5. Read through Isaiah 53 together and discuss how this passage points to Jesus as the Messiah and Savior of the world.

WEEK 3

Born Again

John 3:1–21

By Ellen

I was given up for adoption in 1965. Back then, adoption records were sealed, and birth parents' identities were forever concealed from their children. As an adult, I learned I have two birth certificates. One was created when I was born and contained my biological parents' information. It was secretly stored away. I was then issued a second birth certificate with my adoptive parents' names on it. How incredible that this second birth certificate meant a new life for me with new parents who were overjoyed to welcome me into their family. This week, we will look at an even more remarkable story of spiritual rebirth and the tremendous gifts God has given those who open and receive them.

I invite you to enter into the story of Nicodemus, a man quite different from the ordinary disciples we met last week. Nicodemus was an intellectual scholar and ruler of the Jews, who came to Jesus at night. Nicodemus thought of Jesus as a rabbi of Israel like himself. So, not only did he not understand who Jesus was, but Nicodemus' superior academic training hindered him from understanding what it takes to get to heaven. Let's see how this story unfolds.

WEEK 3 | DAY 1

Seek to Know

Enter into the Story

Prayer

Start your Bible study time with this prayer. Quiet your heart, slow down, and read each word out loud to the Lord:

Dear Lord, please remove any distractions as I study Your Word. Help me to be in awe of the lengths you have gone to give me spiritual rebirth. Amen.

Read slowly and thoughtfully

Open your Bible to John 3:1–21. Read it slowly and thoughtfully. The passage is also included for you here.

Listen to the text while reading

John 3:1–21

You Must Be Born Again

1 Now there was a man of the Pharisees named Nicodemus, a ruler of the
Jews. **2** This man came to Jesus by night and said to him, "Rabbi, we know
that you are a teacher come from God, for no one can do these signs that you
do unless God is with him." **3** Jesus answered him, "Truly, truly, I say to you,
unless one is born again he cannot see the kingdom of God." **4** Nicodemus

said to him, "How can a man be born when he is old? Can he enter a second time into his mother's womb and be born?" **5** Jesus answered, "Truly, truly, I say to you, unless one is born of water and the Spirit, he cannot enter the kingdom of God. **6** That which is born of the flesh is flesh, and that which is born of the Spirit is spirit. **7** Do not marvel that I said to you, 'You must be born again.' **8** The wind blows where it wishes, and you hear its sound, but you do not know where it comes from or where it goes. So it is with everyone who is born of the Spirit."

9 Nicodemus said to him, "How can these things be?" **10** Jesus answered him, "Are you the teacher of Israel and yet you do not understand these things? **11** Truly, truly, I say to you, we speak of what we know, and bear witness to what we have seen, but you do not receive our testimony. **12** If I have told you earthly things and you do not believe, how can you believe if I tell you heavenly things? **13** No one has ascended into heaven except he who descended from heaven, the Son of Man. **14** And as Moses lifted up the serpent in the wilderness, so must the Son of Man be lifted up, **15** that whoever believes in him may have eternal life.

For God So Loved the World

16 "For God so loved the world, that he gave his only Son, that whoever believes in him should not perish but have eternal life. **17** For God did not send his Son into the world to condemn the world, but in order that the world might be saved through him. **18** Whoever believes in him is not condemned, but whoever does not believe is condemned already, because he has not believed in the name of the only Son of God. **19** And this is the judgment: the light has come into the world, and people loved the darkness rather than the light because their works were evil. **20** For everyone who does wicked things hates the light and does not come to the light, lest his works should be exposed. **21** But whoever does what is true comes to the light, so that it may be clearly seen that his works have been carried out in God."

Write down your insights. What stands out to you initially? Also, note any questions you have while reading the text.

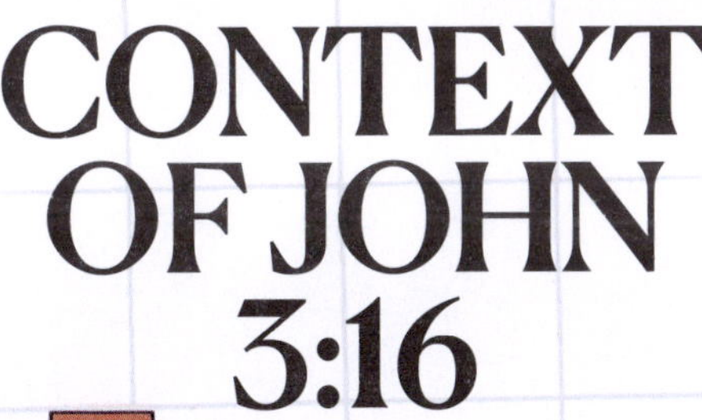

CONTEXT OF JOHN 3:16

A CONVERSATION

John 3:16 appears at the heart of a profound conversation between Jesus and Nicodemus, a respected Pharisee and religious leader. In **verses 1–2**, driven by curiosity, Nicodemus came to Jesus under the cover of night to seek answers about who He truly was.

BEING BORN AGAIN

In verses 3–8, Jesus begins teaching Nicodemus what it truly means to be born again. Though confused, Nicodemus listens as Jesus explains that this new birth is not physical but spiritual—a transformation brought about by the Holy Spirit who gives new life.

JESUS HAS AUTHORITY

In verses 9–13, Jesus explains that He has come from heaven and has the authority to speak about heavenly things—yet Nicodemus still struggles to understand His words.

JESUS POINTS TO THE CROSS

In verses 14–15, Jesus foreshadows the cross by referencing Numbers 21:9. Just as Moses lifted up the bronze serpent so the Israelites could look at it and be healed, Jesus would also be lifted up—and we must look to Him in faith to receive eternal life.

JESUS CAME TO SAVE

In verses 17–21, Jesus explains that He came to save the world, not condemn it. Though He is the light and offers salvation to all, many choose to remain in darkness, rejecting Him—and in doing so, they stand condemned already.

IN SUMMARY

John 3:16 is not a stand-alone verse—it's part of a larger conversation that gives it even greater depth and beauty. Jesus teaches that being born again through the Holy Spirit leads to eternal life, and He alone is the one who gives this new life.

Determine Context

Let's start by investigating the surrounding context before we look directly at the passage's context.

Read John 2:23–25. What does the text say happened that caused many in Jerusalem to believe?

What sign had they just seen Jesus perform in **John 2:1–11**? How did the disciples respond in verse 11?

According to **John 2:24**, record why Jesus does "not entrust himself" to those believers.

Read **Mark 4:1–20**. How does this passage explain why Jesus may not have committed Himself to those believers?

People believed in Jesus because of the miracles He performed. Imagine standing in the crowd and seeing the expression on the face of a blind man the first time he saw light! His face squinted tightly as the sun penetrated his eyes producing unseen images for the very first time. Many witnessed these sensational events firsthand. It's no wonder they initially believed! However, Jesus also knew that **believing in Him because of His miracles was entirely different from trusting in and following Him** as the anticipated Messiah.[8]

In John 3:1–21, John introduces us to Nicodemus, a teacher, Pharisee, and ruler of the Jews. Pharisees lived by the strictest standards of the law,[9] but they often overlooked the heart of the law, such as justice, mercy, and faithfulness, which frequently earned them the label of hypocrites (Matt. 23:13). Like many others, Nicodemus was intrigued by Jesus' miraculous signs, but he could not yet fully understand who Jesus was.

"Truly, truly I say to you, unless one is born again he cannot see the kingdom of heaven."

The sting of Jesus telling Nicodemus that he could not enter the Kingdom of God unless he was born again would have been highly offensive to this well-respected Jewish leader. In Jesus' day, it was thought that all Jews, except those who were guilty of apostasy or extreme wickedness, would be admitted to the Kingdom.[10]

Apostasy

Turning against God, as evidenced by abandonment and repudiation of former beliefs.[11]

Nicodemus may have been a skeptic when he sought out Jesus in the dark of the night to have a private conversation with a man he recognized as having "come from God" (John 3:2). However, by the time Christ was crucified, Nicodemus had a change of heart. Let's look at two passages that lead us to this understanding.

Look up **John 7:40–52**. We read that Jesus had been teaching for several days, and His words captivated the crowds. Some people had favorable opinions of Jesus, for even the temple guards had never heard anyone talk like Him. Still others became enemies. In particular, the Jewish authorities were frustrated by Jesus' rhetoric and jealous of His popularity. They tried unsuccessfully to have Jesus arrested. How did Nicodemus respond? How was he criticized for this response?

Look up **John 19:38–42**. After Jesus' crucifixion, Joseph of Arimathea received permission to take Jesus' body for burial. What did Nicodemus bring, and what did his role in the burial indicate about his view of Jesus?

Jesus was not thrown into a wretched-smelling common criminal grave. Instead, Joseph of Arimathea and Nicodemus, who were both secret disciples, came forward and placed Jesus' body with dignity in a new, garden tomb lavished with sweet-smelling spices fit for a royal burial.[12]

Reflect

Nicodemus was surrounded by a powerful group of leaders who rejected Jesus, yet he reached his own conclusions about Christ. In today's culture, it's easy to be influenced by popular thinking and to care more about people's opinions than God's truth.

How have other people's opinions of Jesus, Scripture, or even the church attempted to influence what you believe? What are some practical things you do to remember God's truth and stand strong in your faith?

WEEK 3 | DAY 2

Spirit, Do a Work in Me

Assess the Main Idea

Now that we have become familiar with John 3:1–21, our goal is to assess the main idea and figure out what this passage means.

Annotate

Reread **John 3:1–21**, but this time focus on key components of the passage. First, be on the lookout for a variety of references to Jesus and Nicodemus. These additional ways of identifying our main characters will lend significant insight into the passage. Additionally, as you read, *notice the themes of being born again, light, eternal life, and belief.* Use the guide below to annotate the passage as you focus on these characters and themes.

Highlight the name **Jesus** and the other **names of Jesus** **in purple**:

- Rabbi, Teacher, Son of Man, Son, Son of God, Light

Highlight the following **character references** **in green**:

- Nicodemus, man of the Pharisees, ruler of the Jews, teacher of Israel

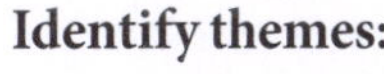

Identify themes:

- Circle the references to **being born again** **in blue**:
    - born again, born, born of water and the spirit, born of the flesh, born of the spirit
- Circle **light in black**
- Circle **eternal life** **in red**
- Highlight any forms of **belief** **in yellow**:
    - believe, believes, believed

Ellen's Annotation Example: **John 3:1–21**

Now there was a man of the Pharisees named Nicodemus, a ruler of the Jews. **2** This man came to Jesus by night and said to him, "Rabbi, we know that you are a teacher come from God, for no one can do these signs that you do unless God is with him." **3** Jesus answered him, "Truly, truly, I say to you, unless one is born again he cannot see the kingdom of God." **4** Nicodemus said to him, "How can a man be born when he is old? Can he enter a second time into his mother's womb and be born?" **5** Jesus answered, "Truly, truly, I say to you, unless one is born of water and the Spirit, he cannot enter the kingdom of God. **6** That which is born of the flesh is flesh, and that which is born of the Spirit is spirit. **7** Do not marvel that I said to you, 'You must be born again.' **8** The wind blows where it wishes, and you hear its sound, but you do not know where it comes from or where it goes. So it is with everyone who is born of the Spirit."

Nicodemus came at night, suggesting that he was in a state of spiritual darkness

Those who inherit the kingdom of God are those who have been born again by the Spirit.

9 Nicodemus said to him, "How can these things be?" **10** Jesus answered him, "Are you the teacher of Israel and yet you do not understand these things? **11** Truly, truly, I say to you, we speak of what we know, and bear witness to what we have seen, but

you do not receive our testimony. **12** If I have told you earthly
things and you do not believe, how can you believe if I tell you
heavenly things? **13** No one has ascended into heaven except
he who descended from heaven, the Son of Man. **14** And as
Moses lifted up the serpent in the wilderness, so must the Son
of Man be lifted up, **15** that whoever believes in him may have
eternal life.

For God So Loved the World

16 "For God so loved the world, that he gave his only Son, that
whoever believes in him should not perish but have eternal life.
17 For God did not send his Son into the world to condemn
the world, but in order that the world might be saved through
him. **18** Whoever believes in him is not condemned, but whoever does not believe is condemned already, because he has not
believed in the name of the only Son of God. **19** And this is the
judgment: the light has come into the world, and people loved
the darkness rather than the light because their works were evil.
20 For everyone who does wicked things hates the light and
does not come to the light, lest his works should be exposed.
21 But whoever does what is true comes to the light, so that it
may be clearly seen that his works have been carried out in God."

Jesus came to give eternal life to whoever believes in Him. "And this is eternal life, that they know you, the only true God, and Jesus Christ whom you have sent." John 17:3

Light is a metaphor for Jesus, who brought the light of truth into the world. People will either love Jesus and follow Him or they will deny Him and persist in their evil ways.

Paraphrase

John 3:1–21 is divided into three sections. I paraphrased the first one for you. Continue paraphrasing the last two sections. Since some of these passages are difficult to paraphrase in only one to two sentences, it is okay to make your summaries longer. You can look back at the passage for help.

John 3:1–8:

We are introduced to Nicodemus. He is one of the Pharisees, a ruler of the Jews. He comes to Jesus at night, wanting to understand the signs that Jesus could not do apart from God.

Jesus tells Nicodemus that he cannot see the Kingdom of God unless he is born again. This confuses Nicodemus, so Jesus explains that rebirth comes from the Spirit.

John 3:9–15:

John 3:16–21:

Main Idea

The main idea of John 3:1–21 is that being born again leads to eternal life. Let's consider what this passage means for us today.

What John shared with his original audience thousands of years ago still holds today. Intellectual knowledge is not enough. Nicodemus, one of Israel's most high-achieving teachers, could not earn his way to heaven. The same is true for us. How much we know or how good we act will not get us into God's Kingdom.

Instead, Nicodemus needed to humble himself, believe, and be born again. We also need this spiritual rebirth, which can only happen through the powerful work of the Spirit. And the good news is that God gave His only Son, so that anyone who believes—which includes Nicodemus and now us—can have eternal life.

Reflect

Through faith in Jesus, we become a part of God's family and receive eternal life. Our adoption begins when we repent of our sins, follow Jesus, and walk in His ways. But eternal life is not just a future reward. We can experience the benefits of it now, too.[13] These benefits come when the Holy Spirit controls our lives. One way we see the evidence of the Holy Spirit in us is through the fruit of the Spirit. Galatians 5:22–23 says, "But the fruit of the Spirit is love, joy, peace, patience, kindness, goodness, faithfulness, gentleness, self-control; against such things there is no law." What's one way you've seen the present reality of eternal life reflected in your everyday life?

WEEK 3 | DAY 3

God Desires You

 Seek God and His Character

Today, we will examine God's incredible qualities in John 3:1–21 by examining explicit and implicit characteristics of God found in the text.

If you are newer to Bible study, be encouraged that Scripture repeatedly makes it clear **who our God is and what He is like**. We just need to take the time to identify God's characteristics in the text and treasure what they mean to us.

Explicit Characteristics of God

Read the verse and draw a line to **match** it to one of the *explicit characteristics of God.*

John 3:2	Jesus is the light that has come into the world.
John 3:5	God is the source of Jesus' authority and power.
John 3:15	God is loving and sent His Son to save the world.
John 3:16	The Spirit is required for spiritual rebirth.
John 3:19	God desires eternal life for whoever believes in Jesus.

Implicit Characteristics of God

Read the verse and draw a line to **match** it to one of the *implicit characteristics of God.*

John 3:11	God is invested in those who come to the light.
John 3:18	God desires to make Himself known.
John 3:21	God is a judge, providing consequences for those who do not believe.

What did you learn about God's love for us?

How would you describe what it means to be born again to someone?

How does God's desire to make Himself known to you touch your heart?

Jesus wanted Nicodemus to come to the light, just as God wants each of us to seek truth and righteousness and find Him. God does not force us to love Him. In fact, He gives us the free will to either choose or reject Jesus as our Lord and Savior. It wouldn't be love if God didn't give us this choice. However, one day, *every person will face God as the ultimate Judge*, with belief in His Son the determining factor for receiving eternal life.

Journal

Nicodemus addressed his inner skepticism about who Jesus really was by going directly to Him and verbalizing his thoughts and confusion. Maybe you too have struggled with something related to God's character and in time you learned to trust that God is who He says He is. Journal about one of those experiences, thanking God for the work He has done in your life.

Close your time in prayer, praising God for who He is.

WEEK 3 | DAY 4

Walk in the Light

Yearn for a Heart Change and Deeper Intimacy with God

This week, we have been studying Jesus' late-night conversation with Nicodemus about his need for spiritual rebirth. As the two talked, Jesus emphatically declared, "Truly, truly, I say to you, unless one is born again he cannot enter the kingdom of God" (John 3:5). Even though this Pharisee saw Jesus' extraordinary signs with his physical eyes, he spiritually could not see and was not ready to follow Jesus as the promised Messiah.[14]

Yet Jesus took the time to guide Nicodemus through a series of illustrations, instructing him in the basics of salvation so that he could be spiritually reborn. Jesus wanted Nicodemus to come to know the Savior directly in his midst. He wants this for you as well.

Inward Transformation

Spiritual rebirth or being "born again" (John 3:3) is **a one-time occurrence when the Holy Spirit enters us**, opens your eyes to the truth, and causes us to experience spiritual transformation. What circumstances did God use to make you aware of your need for a Savior and put your faith and trust in Jesus Christ? Write out your testimony to remind yourself of how God has been at work in your life and so that you will always be prepared to share your story.

Testimony

- A testimony reflects your personal story of how God has been at work in your life.
- A helpful way to get started is by creating a timeline of your life. Note these:
    - Spiritual heritage from great-grandparents forward
    - Wonders surrounding your birth
    - People who planted the early seeds of Christian belief
    - Challenges that impacted your walk with God
    - Blessings that impacted your walk with God
    - The date you accepted Christ as your personal savior
    - The date you were baptized
- Turn this into a short story of God's victory in your life.

Outward Application

Believing in Jesus involves more than head knowledge or merely comprehending what Scripture says. Nicodemus was intellectual and considered a great teacher of Israel, yet he didn't understand how to be saved. He had to learn that **the Spirit transforms us** from the head to the heart, and it's then that we begin to live out our faith by following Jesus. We do this by reading the Bible, praying and worshiping God, and loving and serving others. What steps are you taking to follow Jesus and grow spiritually?

In John 3:19, Jesus says that "the light has come into the world, but people loved the darkness rather than the light." Another way we follow Jesus is by loving the light rather than the darkness. But what does that mean? Walking in darkness is when we decide to choose our own way instead of following what God tells us is right. For example, when you feel the prompting of the Holy Spirit not to share or listen to the latest bit of gossip, but you brush it aside and join the conversation anyway, that is disregarding Scripture's instruction to avoid gossip (Prov. 20:19; 16:28). However tempting it might be to bond with others through gossip, God wants us to *walk in the light* by guarding our words and using them to point others to Him.

Read 1 John 1:5–10. In what ways does this passage deepen your understanding of what it means to walk in the light?

What kinds of social pressures are you currently facing? Which ones do you tend to give in to, and what are some practical ways you can choose to walk in the light instead?

Is there anything God has laid on your heart to let go of so that you can let your light shine to the world?

Based on John 3:16, what do you infer for those who do not believe? How heavy does that weigh on your heart for unbelievers in your life? How are you being a witness for Christ?

Be encouraged, friend, that God loves you so much that He sent His one and only Son to die on a cross for you so that you might be saved. Now that's good news!

WEEK 3 | DAY 5

Our Eternity Is Secure

Dig Deeper

DIG DEEPER

Today, we will dig deeper into John 3:1–21 by further annotating the passage to see what we learn about the triune God: Father, Son, and Holy Spirit. We will also examine what this week's passage reminds us about God's Kingdom, both now and in the future.

Annotate

Pull out your annotated passage from Day 2 of this week. You have already highlighted all of the references to the Son of God in green. Now, continue to make the following annotations:

Highlight all references to **God the Father in orange**:

- God, He, His

Highlight all references to the **Holy Spirit in blue**:

- Spirit

Highlight all references to the Trinity **in pink**:

- we, our

Ellen's Annotation Example: **John 3:1–21**

Now there was a man of the Pharisees named Nicodemus, a
ruler of the Jews. **2** This man came to Jesus by night and said to
him, "Rabbi, we know that you are a teacher come from God, for
no one can do these signs that you do unless God is with him."
3 Jesus answered him, "Truly, truly, I say to you, unless one
is born again he cannot see the kingdom of God." **4** Nicodemus
said to him, "How can a man be born when he is old? Can he
enter a second time into his mother's womb and be born?"
5 Jesus answered, "Truly, truly, I say to you, unless one is born
of water and the Spirit, he cannot enter the kingdom of God.
6 That which is born of the flesh is flesh, and that which is born
of the Spirit is spirit. **7** Do not marvel that I said to you, 'You
must be born again.' **8** The wind blows where it wishes, and you
hear its sound, but you do not know where it comes from or
where it goes. So it is with everyone who is born of the Spirit."

9 Nicodemus said to him, "How can these things be?" **10** Jesus
answered him, "Are you the teacher of Israel and yet you do not
understand these things? **11** Truly, truly, I say to you, we speak
of what we know, and bear witness to what we have seen, but

you do not receive our testimony. **12** If I have told you earthly
things and you do not believe, how can you believe if I tell you
heavenly things? **13** No one has ascended into heaven except
he who descended from heaven, the Son of Man. **14** And as
Moses lifted up the serpent in the wilderness, so must the Son
of Man be lifted up, **15** that whoever believes in him may have
eternal life.

For God So Loved the World

16 "For God so loved the world, that he gave his only Son, that
whoever believes in him should not perish but have eternal life.
17 For God did not send his Son into the world to condemn
the world, but in order that the world might be saved through
him. **18** Whoever believes in him is not condemned, but whoever does not believe is condemned already, because he has not
believed in the name of the only Son of God. **19** And this is the
judgment: the light has come into the world, and people loved
the darkness rather than the light because their works were evil.
20 For everyone who does wicked things hates the light and
does not come to the light, lest his works should be exposed.
21 But whoever does what is true comes to the light, so that it
may be clearly seen that his works have been carried out in God."

What does the text say about God the Father?

What does the text say about God the Son?

What does the text say about God the Holy Spirit?

What does the text say about the Trinity?

What did you learn from this exercise that expands your understanding of each person of the Holy Trinity and how they are one?

God the Father loved the world so He gave Jesus, His only Son. The Light of the World, Jesus, was lifted up on a cross to bear your sins and mine so that we can receive eternal life. And Jesus Himself said the Spirit cannot be seen (John 3:8), yet is instrumental in us being born again. When we have the Holy Spirit within us, darkness is lifted so that we can see the light.

Kingdom of God

Present	Future
• Limited on earth • Christ came and paid the price for sin • The Spirit dwells within us • Holiness is growing in us • Sin, Satan and death defeated, yet still a battle • Power to endure suffering • Peace and joy	• Fully in heaven • Christ will come again to rule and reign • Live in unity with God • Sin defeated • Perfect bodies • Eternal life • No more suffering • Righteousness

John 3:1–21 is driving us to see the great **gift** God has in store for us now and in the future **if we believe**. While we are here on earth, we rarely take time to consider that our lives are but a dot on a page, and all of eternity is a line that extends to infinity.

We can enjoy some of the benefits of God's Kingdom today. The Holy Spirit works in us to battle against our sinfulness and choose God's ways instead of our own. Every day, we have His help to grow in holiness and the fruit of the Spirit. His strength allows us to patiently endure suffering, and His peace comforts us in our pain.

But in the future Kingdom of God, we will enjoy every benefit—not just some. We will live in the presence of God in perfected bodies that will no longer endure pain or suffering and will last for all eternity. That sounds pretty good to me! How about you?

Reflect

Now write a prayer of reflection and praise to God about your eternity.

The Journey Continues

Next week, we will shift our attention from Nicodemus, a highly respected Jewish moral leader who didn't know how to enter the Kingdom of heaven, to an outcast Samaritan woman who was plagued with the same problem. The contrast between their genders and socioeconomic statuses could not be more different, but their need was the same. They both needed Jesus.

Stay engaged as we pivot to this woman who changed her community and the world. She encountered the living Christ at an unexpected meeting at a well on the outskirts of town. But her clay jar was not the only thing that was filled that day. Her heart was filled with the Holy Spirit, making her the first reported woman evangelist in the gospel. Next week, we will dive deep into her story!

Discussion Questions

To help you reflect on the week of study, here are optional discussion questions that you can discuss with a friend, mentor, or small group.

1. What is significant about Nicodemus coming to Jesus?
2. How does Jesus teach Nicodemus the idea of being born again? What does it mean?
3. What bold claims does Jesus make about Himself in this passage?
4. Which themes (born again, eternal life, condemnation, light and darkness) resonated most with you and why?
5. What do you think eternal life will be like in the Kingdom of God? See Revelation 21:21–25, 1 Corinthians 2:9, Philippians 3:20–21, and Matthew 6:19–21.

WEEK 4

He Knows Me!

John 4:1–42

By Ellen

Have you ever had a teacher notice you? When I was in school, I rarely interacted with my teachers. I tried to stay unnoticed. One teacher, however, spoke into my life. It was my sewing instructor. She noticed me and saw something in me that I could not see in myself.

My grandma had already taught me the basics of sewing. So, while the other girls were making skirts, my sewing instructor encouraged me to take on a more challenging project. I grew my skills by making a bright green down ski vest, complete with three zippers and snaps. This teacher saw me, listened to me, and spoke encouraging words to me that have lasted a lifetime.

The Samaritan woman in John 4 also kept to herself and tried to stay unnoticed. She sought water at the hottest part of the day when no one else would be there. But on one particular day, someone was there—Jesus. He saw her, listened to her, and spoke truth into her life. Although she sought to fill her immediate need for water in a single jar, Jesus was about to give her a lifetime supply. Let's travel to Samaria and enter into her story.

WEEK 4 | DAY 1

Travel to Samaria

Enter into the Story

Prayer

Start your Bible study time with this prayer. Quiet your heart, slow down, and read each word out loud to the Lord:

Dear Lord, please remove any distractions as I study Your Word. Thank You that You see me, know me, hear me, and love me. Amen.

Read slowly and thoughtfully

Open your Bible to John 4:1–42. Read it slowly and thoughtfully. The passage is also included for you here.

Listen to the text while reading

John 4:1–42

Jesus and the Woman of Samaria

1 Now when Jesus learned that the Pharisees had heard that Jesus was making and baptizing more disciples than John **2** (although Jesus himself did not
baptize, but only his disciples), **3** he left Judea and departed again for Galilee.
4 And he had to pass through Samaria. **5** So he came to a town of Samaria
called Sychar, near the field that Jacob had given to his son Joseph. **6** Jacob's
well was there; so Jesus, wearied as he was from his journey, was sitting beside
the well. It was about the sixth hour.

7 A woman from Samaria came to draw water. Jesus said to her, "Give me a drink." **8** (For his disciples had gone away into the city to buy food.) **9** The Samaritan woman said to him, "How is it that you, a Jew, ask for a drink from me, a woman of Samaria?" (For Jews have no dealings with Samaritans.) **10** Jesus answered her, "If you knew the gift of God, and who it is that is saying to you, 'Give me a drink,' you would have asked him, and he would have given you living water." **11** The woman said to him, "Sir, you have nothing to draw water with, and the well is deep. Where do you get that living water? **12** Are you greater than our father Jacob? He gave us the well and drank from it himself, as did his sons and his livestock." **13** Jesus said to her, "Everyone who drinks of this water will be thirsty again, **14** but whoever drinks of the water that I will give him will never be thirsty again. The water that I will give him will become in him a spring of water welling up to eternal life." **15** The woman said to him, "Sir, give me this water, so that I will not be thirsty or have to come here to draw water."

16 Jesus said to her, "Go, call your husband, and come here." **17** The woman answered him, "I have no husband." Jesus said to her, "You are right in saying, 'I have no husband'; **18** for you have had five husbands, and the one you now have is not your husband. What you have said is true." **19** The woman said to him, "Sir, I perceive that you are a prophet. **20** Our fathers worshiped on this mountain, but you say that in Jerusalem is the place where people ought to worship." **21** Jesus said to her, "Woman, believe me, the hour is coming when neither on this mountain nor in Jerusalem will you worship the Father. **22** You worship what you do not know; we worship what we know, for salvation is from the Jews. **23** But the hour is coming, and is now here, when the true worshipers will worship the Father in spirit and truth, for the Father is seeking such people to worship him. **24** God is spirit, and those who worship him must worship in spirit and truth." **25** The woman said to him, "I know that Messiah is coming (he who is called Christ). When he comes, he will tell us all things." **26** Jesus said to her, "I who speak to you am he."

27 Just then his disciples came back. They marveled that he was talking with

a woman, but no one said, "What do you seek?" or, "Why are you talking with
her?" **28** So the woman left her water jar and went away into town and said to
the people, **29** "Come, see a man who told me all that I ever did. Can this be
the Christ?" **30** They went out of the town and were coming to him.

31 Meanwhile the disciples were urging him, saying, "Rabbi, eat." **32** But
he said to them, "I have food to eat that you do not know about." **33** So the
disciples said to one another, "Has anyone brought him something to eat?"
34 Jesus said to them, "My food is to do the will of him who sent me and to
accomplish his work. **35** Do you not say, 'There are yet four months, then
comes the harvest'? Look, I tell you, lift up your eyes, and see that the fields
are white for harvest. **36** Already the one who reaps is receiving wages and
gathering fruit for eternal life, so that sower and reaper may rejoice together.
37 For here the saying holds true, 'One sows and another reaps.' **38** I sent you
to reap that for which you did not labor. Others have labored, and you have
entered into their labor."

39 Many Samaritans from that town believed in him because of the woman's
testimony, "He told me all that I ever did." **40** So when the Samaritans came
to him, they asked him to stay with them, and he stayed there two days.
41 And many more believed because of his word. **42** They said to the woman,
"It is no longer because of what you said that we believe, for we have heard for
ourselves, and we know that this is indeed the Savior of the world."

Write down your insights. What stands out to you initially? Also, note any questions you have while reading the text.

Put yourself in the story

Today, you will immerse yourself in Samaritan culture and explore context clues by placing yourself in the scene where Jesus meets the woman at the well.

Imagine walking alongside Jesus and His disciples, traveling from Judea to Galilee through Samaria on foot. As a local back then, you may be surprised that Jesus chooses to go through the land of the Samaritans, whom the Jews hate. After all, you know that a different route to Galilee would eliminate the trek through Samaria. What you don't know yet is that Jesus has a divine appointment in the town of Sychar.

This three-day journey encompasses over seventy miles of rugged rock roads in a hot, dry climate.[15] Your face is beet red from the heat, your body is sweating, and your mouth is parched dry—my, what you wouldn't give for a drink of water! Are you there yet? You're relieved when the tired and sore feet of Jesus take refuge during the heat of the noonday sun at Jacob's well. Finally, a water break! And it's this stop that sets the scene for what will unfold in the rest of the story.

Jesus' trip to Samaria was His first mission outside Jewish territory and represented the start of a cross-cultural mission from God.[16] Not only did Jesus cross this **ethnic** boundary, but He also moved past **religious** and **gender** barriers.

History of the Samaritans[17]

- The Assyrians captured Samaria in 722–721 BC.
- Many Jews were deported while some remained in Samaria.
- Surviving Israelites in Samaria intermarried with foreigners and took part in aspects of their religion.
- The Jews who were deported viewed the Samaritans as half-breeds who had been tainted by other religious beliefs.
- In 400 BC, the Samaritans built their own temple on Mount Gerizim, rivaling the Jewish temple in Jerusalem.
- All of these events contributed to the animosity between the Jews and Samaritans.

Determine Context

Read the history of the Samaritans in the text box and then look up **John 4:9** and **4:27**. What do you learn about ethnic and cultural divisions from the text?

Barry J. Beitzel, *The Moody Bible Atlas* (Chicago: Moody, 2025)

The map of Jesus' travels from Galilee to Jerusalem is a helpful reference for this week's lesson. Circle Mount Gerizim and the cities of Sychar and Jerusalem on the map. The rift between the Jews and Samaritans resulted in the Samaritans building their temple for worship on Mount Gerizim. They determined that this was the proper place of worship, as Abraham had built an altar there when he first entered the promised land. Meanwhile, the Jews held to honoring King David's designated place of worship in Jerusalem. Tomorrow, we will see how Jesus sorts out these conflicting religious claims.[18]

Another vital context clue related to this passage involves an additional natural element in our scene. Our gospel writer, John, repeatedly uses the theme of water, and this story is no exception. This time, we find ourselves at a well where we learn that our basic need for water runs deeper than our physical thirst. Look up the following words in an online dictionary:

Well:

Spring:

We see the contrast between a well, a deep human-made reservoir dug in the ground that requires repeated labor to pull water from it, and a spring, a place where water flows freely and is readily available coming up from underground.[19] Store these images in your mind for tomorrow, when we will drink deeper into Jesus' spring of water.

"The water that I will give him will become in him a spring of water welling up to eternal life."

Now that you have stepped into the story by feeling the bumpy rocks under your leather sandals and swatting at bugs in the heat of the day, you are one step closer to gaining a richer viewpoint of the woman at the well story. Next, we will jump right into assessing the main idea.

WEEK 4 | DAY 2

Live for Him

Assess the Main Idea

Annotate

Now that we have become familiar with John 4:1–42, our goal is to assess the main idea and figure out what this passage means.

Reread John 4:1–42, but this time focus on some key components of the passage. Alert yourself to multiple names of Jesus and the Samaritan woman. Also, as you read, *pay attention to the themes of water and thirst, Jesus crossing barriers, worship, and belief*. Use the guide below to annotate the passage as you focus on these characters and themes.

Highlight the name **Jesus** and the other **names of Jesus** **in purple**:

- Jew, prophet, Messiah, Christ, I who speak to you am he, Rabbi, Savior

Highlight the following **character references** **in green**:

- Woman from Samaria, Samaritan woman, woman of Samaria, woman('s)

Identify themes:

- Circle the symbolisms of **water and thirst** **in blue**:
  - Well, water, drink(s), living water, drank, thirsty, spring of water
- Underline the places where **Jesus crosses ethnic, religious, and gender boundaries** **in orange**:
  - John 4:4, 4:7, 4:9, 4:22, 4:27, 4:39

- Circle the concept of **worshiping in spirit and truth** in red:
    - Worship, worshiped, worshipers, spirit, truth
- Highlight any formats of **belief** in yellow:
    - Believe, believed

Ellen's Annotation Example: John 4:1–42

1 Now when Jesus learned that the Pharisees had heard
that Jesus was making and baptizing more disciples than John
2 (although Jesus himself did not baptize, but only his disciples),
3 he left Judea and departed again for Galilee. **4** And he had to
pass through Samaria. **5** So he came to a town of Samaria called
Sychar, near the field that Jacob had given to his son Joseph.
6 Jacob's well was there; so Jesus, wearied as he was from his
journey, was sitting beside the well. It was about the sixth hour.
7 A woman from Samaria came to draw water. Jesus said to
her, "Give me a drink." **8** (For his disciples had gone away into
the city to buy food.) **9** The Samaritan woman said to him,
"How is it that you, a Jew, ask for a drink from me, a woman of
Samaria?" (For Jews have no dealings with Samaritans.) **10** Jesus
answered her, "If you knew the gift of God, and who it is that
is saying to you, 'Give me a drink,' you would have asked him,
and he would have given you living water." **11** The woman said
to him, "Sir, you have nothing to draw water with, and the well

Jesus crosses ethnic, religious, and gender boundaries

is deep. Where do you get that living water? **12** Are you greater
than our father Jacob? He gave us the well and drank from it
himself, as did his sons and his livestock." **13** Jesus said to her,
"Everyone who drinks of this water will be thirsty again, **14** but
whoever drinks of the water that I will give him will never be
thirsty again. The water that I will give him will become in him a
spring of water welling up to eternal life." **15** The woman said to
him, "Sir, give me this water, so that I will not be thirsty or have
to come here to draw water."

The water that Jesus offers leads to eternal life

16 Jesus said to her, "Go, call your husband, and come here."
17 The woman answered him, "I have no husband." Jesus said
to her, "You are right in saying, 'I have no husband'; **18** for you
have had five husbands, and the one you now have is not your
husband. What you have said is true." **19** The woman said to
him, "Sir, I perceive that you are a prophet. **20** Our fathers
worshiped on this mountain, but you say that in Jerusalem is
the place where people ought to worship." **21** Jesus said to her,
"Woman, believe me, the hour is coming when neither on this
mountain nor in Jerusalem will you worship the Father. **22** You
worship what you do not know; we worship what we know, for
salvation is from the Jews. **23** But the hour is coming, and is now
here, when the true worshipers will worship the Father in spirit

True worship is not about the place. It means having a heart that seeks a personal relationship with God, who is spirit, and worships Him through Christ, guided by the truth of His Word.

and truth, for the Father is seeking such people to worship him.
24 God is spirit, and those who worship him must worship in
spirit and truth." **25** The woman said to him, "I know that Messiah
is coming (he who is called Christ). When he comes, he will tell us
all things." **26** Jesus said to her, "I who speak to you am he."

27 Just then his disciples came back. They marveled that he was
talking with a woman, but no one said, "What do you seek?"
or, "Why are you talking with her?" **28** So the woman left her
water jar and went away into town and said to the people, **29**
"Come, see a man who told me all that I ever did. Can this be the
Christ?" **30** They went out of the town and were coming to him.

31 Meanwhile the disciples were urging him, saying, "Rabbi,
eat." **32** But he said to them, "I have food to eat that you do not
know about." **33** So the disciples said to one another, "Has anyone brought him something to eat?" **34** Jesus said to them, "My
food is to do the will of him who sent me and to accomplish his
work. **35** Do you not say, 'There are yet four months, then comes
the harvest'? Look, I tell you, lift up your eyes, and see that the
fields are white for harvest. **36** Already the one who reaps is
receiving wages and gathering fruit for eternal life, so that sower
and reaper may rejoice together. **37** For here the saying holds
true, 'One sows and another reaps.' **38** I sent you to reap that

for which you did not labor. Others have labored, and you have
entered into their labor.”
39 Many Samaritans from that town believed in him because
of the woman’s testimony, “He told me all that I ever did.”
40 So when the Samaritans came to him, they asked him to stay
with them, and he stayed there two days. **41** And many more
believed because of his word. **42** They said to the woman, “It is
no longer because of what you said that we believe, for we have
heard for ourselves, and we know that this is indeed the Savior
of the world.”

Many Samaritans believed in Jesus because of the woman’s outreach and Jesus’ words

Paraphrase

John 4:1–42 is divided into four sections so you can create your paraphrases. I paraphrased the first one for you. Continue with your paraphrases of the last three sections. If you need help or want to see how you did, an answer key is provided in the back of the book.

John 4:1–9:

Despite cross-cultural barriers, Jesus has a divine appointment to pass through Samaria, where He meets the Samaritan woman. After traveling in the heat of the day, Jesus asks the woman for a drink. She is shocked that He would ask her because Jews have no dealings with Samaritans.

John 4:10–15:

John 4:16–26:

John 4:27–41:

THE SAMARITAN WOMAN'S

ROAD TO BELIEF

1 JESUS SEEKS HER

- Woman endures laborious task of drawing water from a well (John 4:7)
- She avoids people by doing this during the heat of the day (John 4:6)
- Jesus takes the long road to intentionally cross her path (John 4:3–5)

2 JESUS CROSSES BOUNDARIES FOR HER

- Jesus, a Jew, passes through Samaria and asks a Samaritan woman for a drink (John 4:7–9, 27)

3 JESUS OFFERS LIVING WATER TO HER

- Jesus offers her living water so she will not thirst again (John 4:10–14)
- The water Jesus offers leads to eternal life (John 4:14)

4 JESUS KNOWS HER

- Jesus tells her she has had five husbands and is currently with another man (John 4:16–18, 29, 39)
- She tells her town about Jesus and they believe in him because of her testimony (John 4:28–30, 39)

5 JESUS REVEALS HIMSELF TO HER

- Jesus tells her He is the Messiah about whom she speaks (John 4:25–26)
- Jesus stays for two extra days in their town and many more believe in Him (John 4:40–42)

Main Idea

Now that you have paraphrased these verses, let's pull out the key themes so that we can assess the main idea. I completed the first one for you as an example. Write a one to two-sentence summary of each of these key themes.

Water and thirst:

Yesterday, we looked up the definitions of **well** and **spring**. The woman learns that the unending *laborious task* of acquiring the water from Jacob's well would only *temporarily satisfy* her thirst. But the *freely available* water Jesus provides is a spring of life-giving water welling up to *eternal life*.

Jesus crosses ethnic, religious, and gender boundaries:

Worshiping God in spirit and truth:

Belief in Jesus:

Reflect

Jesus loves us and truly knows us. He knows our every **thought** and all of the **details** of our lives before we put our trust in Him. And, despite our shortcomings, He wants us to follow Him so that we can experience the life-giving water that only He can offer.

Reflect on your inner character and how Jesus knows every facet of your being. How does that inspire you to live for Him and share the gospel, just as the Samaritan woman did?

WEEK 4 | DAY 3

Run to Jesus

Seek God and His Character

Today, we will explore some explicit and implicit qualities of God found in John 4:1–42. This passage continues a series of conversations in which Jesus disclosed Himself as the fulfillment of the Old Testament prophecies. Let's take a closer look at the ways He did this.

Read

Reread John 4:1–42.

Explicit Characteristics of God

Fill in the blanks with the *explicit* characteristics of God. To further your understanding, read the added commentary about each quality.

Jesus is a J ____________ (John 4:9).

- Jesus came from a Jewish lineage, lived and worked in the Jewish communities of Galilee and Judea, and had a Jewish name, Jeshua.

Jesus gives l ____________ w ____________ (John 4:10).

- Jesus provides spiritual fulfillment and eternal life. After Christ's death, resurrection, and ascension to heaven, and His glorification, He gave all believers the outpouring of the Holy Spirit.

Jesus is a p________________ (John 4:19).

- Jesus is considered the ultimate prophet (Acts 3:22–23). He foretold future events, spoke inspired messages from God, and offered Himself as the ultimate sacrifice. He is the sinless incarnate Son of God.

God the Father is w________________ in s________________ and t________________ (John 4:23).

- *God is worthy of our worship*. Worshiping in spirit and truth is a matter of the heart. We are to love God with all our heart, soul, and might (Deut. 6:5). It is not disingenuous lip service. God is *omnipresent* (we'll define this in a couple of pages) and can be worshiped anywhere at any time.

God is s________________ (John 4:24).

- God the Father does not have a visible form. Although He is not made up of matter He does have power. He is not from the same order as human beings.

Jesus is the M________________ who is called C________________ (John 4:25–26).

- This is one of the "I Am" statements in the gospel of John, where Jesus explicitly identifies Himself as the Messiah, the "Anointed One" in Hebrew. Jesus is the Savior of the world, the long-awaited Jewish Anointed One that the Israelites were waiting for.

Jesus is the R________________ (John 4:31).

- Back on Week 2, Day 3, we talked about how *rabbi* means teacher. To review, usually, rabbis taught the law and had students or disciples who followed them closely.

Jesus' mission is to d___ the w______ of Him who sent Him (John 4:34).

- Jesus is committed to doing the Father's will, sacrificing Himself to provide salvation for all believers. His work on the cross bears witness to His divine mission.

Jesus is the S____________________ of the world (John 4:42).

- Jesus offers salvation to **everyone** regardless of religious background, nationality, or gender. He **does not discriminate** in any way.

Implicit Characteristics of God

Describe in your own words the *implicit* characteristics of God. Take time to determine what the text is implying.

John 4:16–18

Omniscience

The divine attribute of infinite knowledge and understanding of things past, present, and future.[20]

Jesus is all-knowing or *omniscient*, as exemplified by His understanding of the woman's detailed past without ever meeting her. He could read her heart and knew she needed a Savior.

John 4:41–42

Omnipotence

The divine attribute of absolute power and authority to bring into existence or cause to happen whatsoever He will.[21]

Jesus spoke from a place of authority from His Father, revealing divine *omnipotence* as the Son of God. We see this in the miraculous conversion of Samaritans brought about by His very word, which caused them to believe.

"He told me all I ever did."

Reflect

Take time to review each of these explicit and implicit characteristics. We can almost see the wheels turning in the Samaritan woman's head as she picks up on the omniscience of Jesus in John 4:29. Her excitement prevails as she proclaims to the people in her town, "Come, see a man who told me all that I ever did. Can this be the Christ?" (John 4:39).

How have you experienced one or more of these character traits in your life this week?

Friend, I hope you see God's extraordinary love for you by now. He desires for you to grow in relationship with Him beginning here on **earth** and extending throughout all **eternity**. He is compassionate and gracious, meaning you can run to Him with expectant mercy. Keep abiding in Him one day at a time.

WEEK 4 | DAY 4

Take Your Faith on the Road

Yearn for a Heart Change and Deeper Intimacy with God

There's great excitement in this passage as we see the Samaritan woman, in the desert heat, go from her mundane task of drawing water from a well to her realization that she has met the promised Messiah, who knows the very depths of her soul. It was a discovery that she could not keep to herself. So inspired was the woman that she led an **evangelistic outreach** in her community, causing a ripple effect in others' beliefs.

Inward Transformation

God used the Samaritan woman's encounter at the well with Jesus to **transform her heart**, and He wants to transform yours too. Let's look at some factors that can lead to inward transformation.

Jesus could see that the Samaritan woman was thirsting for something that could not satisfy. He gently called her out for having five husbands and being with yet another man. He redirects her to finding soul-level nourishment exclusively in Him.

How might Jesus lovingly challenge you today, as He did with the Samaritan woman?

How are culture or those around you who aren't following Jesus trying to persuade you to thirst for things that don't satisfy your soul? What are a few practical ways you can stay focused on Jesus and thirsting for the living water He gives?

Jesus said His food was to do the will of the Father. We learn what God's will is when we study Scripture and obediently live it out. Is doing God's will as vital to you as eating food? If not, how can you seek to make obeying Him your first priority?

Jesus told the Samaritan woman that God is seeking true worshipers who worship in spirit and truth. The truth has been revealed through Jesus' life and in God's Word, and the Holy Spirit fills all believers with a desire to worship Him. How has God used the woman at the well passage this week to reveal His truth to you? How has it impacted your desire to worship Him?

Outward Application

God also wants us to **actively live out** what we learn in His Word and love others as Jesus does. Consider the questions below as opportunities to take your faith on the road.

When you share your faith, do you feel the same excitement and awe that the Samaritan woman felt when she told people about Jesus? If not, what are some practical ways you can reawaken that feeling?

Jesus crossed cultural barriers and lived without prejudice. How can you do the same in your community and spheres of influence?

The Samaritan woman came to faith through a progression of interactions with Jesus. She first saw Jesus as simply another Jew, then she suspected He was a prophet, and ultimately, the Christ. Jesus was patient and did not force understanding upon her. In today's instant gratification society, we want everything immediately, especially to see our family and friends decide to follow Jesus. God's timing, however, is not always our timing. He has a plan and purpose for when and how others accept His Son as their Savior.

Write down five people God has put on your heart that don't know Him yet. Pray for God's salvation in their lives and patience in yours as you wait on His timing.

1. ______________________________

2. ______________________________

3. ______________________________

4. ______________________________

5. ______________________________

In John's story of the woman at the well, we met a Samaritan woman who didn't realize she needed heart change. She believed she needed physical water. Yet, **inward transformation** was exactly what she found when she met Jesus at the well. We witness how her faith journey began, how her intimacy with Jesus grew, and what she accomplished for God's Kingdom as a result. But she's not the only woman Jesus wants to transform from the inside out. He wants to do that for you too! Do you see Him at work in your life? Friend, He is there. He is working. So, be encouraged and keep yearning for Him.

WEEK 4 | DAY 5

Never Thirst Again

Digging Deeper

DIG DEEPER **Read John 4:13–14.** Today, you will have additional time to seek God and His character. You will be given a variety of options to choose from to help you meditate on these verses. Select a way that resonates with you.

Option #1: Prayer
Pray over the verses, focusing on praising God for His gift of life-giving water and eternal life.

Option #2: Journaling
Write down your response to God's gift of life-giving water through means of poetry, songwriting, a letter to God, or a simple journal entry.

Option #3: Art
Meditate on John 4:13–14 and allow it to inspire a sketch, painting, or collage.

Option #4: Worship
Scripture has inspired music writers since the Bible began. These artists have a way of helping us worship by bringing the verses to life through thought-provoking lyrics and beautiful instrumentation. For example, search for and listen to Olivia Lane's contemporary song titled "Woman at the Well."[22] Then reflect on the parts of the song that resonate with you.

The Journey Continues

If you are broken-hearted, feeling isolated, or struggling, remember that like the woman at the well, **Jesus knows you**! There are no hidden secrets or past mistakes you carry that are too large for His grace to cover. He has already begun to transform you by making Himself known to you. Now share with others the story of what He is doing in your life with the eager heart of the Samaritan woman.

Next week, we continue our journey in John. You will be intrigued by a miracle that serves to tell the world that Jesus' light shines in the darkness. A healed blind man came to recognize Jesus as the Son of Man, yet ironically, the Pharisees with physical sight and scriptural knowledge were spiritually blind.

Discussion Questions

To help you reflect on the week of study, here are optional discussion questions that you can discuss with a friend, mentor, or small group.

1. How are the woman at the well and Nicodemus similar? How are they different?
2. Based on what you learned about the Samaritans and Jesus' intentional pass through their village, what can you conclude about the types of people that Jesus came to seek and save?
3. What is significant about Jesus choosing this woman as the first person He reveals Himself to as the Messiah?
4. The woman leaves her water jar and runs to town to share the news about Jesus. What symbolism might the woman have in leaving her jar at the well?
5. Who might God be prompting you to share the good news with this week?

WEEK 5

Spiritual Blindness

John 9:1–41

By Taylor

I'm jealous of your faith," a new friend unexpectedly confessed. As a recent PhD graduate, she loved to debate passionately on topics related to science. "I live off of science, numbers, and data. I cannot get past that! Now, if I could just *see* the proof and know for certain that God exists, I think then I could finally believe."

When I brought Scripture into the conversation, she recoiled. We argued over the origins of the universe, debating whether it was the result of God or the Big Bang.

"Doesn't it require *more* faith to believe that the universe suddenly appeared?" I gently inquired. "I thought all scientists agreed that something cannot be made from nothing?"

She conceded my point, leaving our conversation with the same words she began with, "While I am jealous of your simple faith, I just can't believe without seeing."

This week, you will study John 9:1–41, where Jesus brings sight to a blind man. This man didn't just undergo an outward transformation; he also experienced a spiritual one. Yet, even when individuals around him witnessed the visible proof of God's power, they still chose unbelief. And ironically, the people who became the most obsessed with the miracle were the least likely to truly see God.

WEEK 5 | DAY 1

Healed on the Sabbath

Enter into the Story

Prayer

Start your Bible study time with this prayer. Quiet your heart, slow down, and read each word out loud to the Lord:

Dear Lord, open my eyes to see Your healing power and soften my heart to embrace who You are. Amen.

Read slowly and thoughtfully

Open your Bible to John 9:1–41. Read it slowly and thoughtfully. The passage is also included for you here.

Listen to the text while reading

John 9:1–41

Jesus Heals a Man Born Blind

1 As he passed by, he saw a man blind from birth. **2** And his disciples asked
him, "Rabbi, who sinned, this man or his parents, that he was born blind?"
3 Jesus answered, "It was not that this man sinned, or his parents, but that the
works of God might be displayed in him. **4** We must work the works of him
who sent me while it is day; night is coming, when no one can work. **5** As long
as I am in the world, I am the light of the world." **6** Having said these things, he
spit on the ground and made mud with the saliva. Then he anointed the man's

eyes with the mud **7** and said to him, "Go, wash in the pool of Siloam" (which means Sent). So he went and washed and came back seeing.

8 The neighbors and those who had seen him before as a beggar were saying, "Is this not the man who used to sit and beg?" **9** Some said, "It is he." Others said, "No, but he is like him." He kept saying, "I am the man." **10** So they said to him, "Then how were your eyes opened?" **11** He answered, "The man called Jesus made mud and anointed my eyes and said to me, 'Go to Siloam and wash.' So I went and washed and received my sight." **12** They said to him, "Where is he?" He said, "I do not know."

13 They brought to the Pharisees the man who had formerly been blind. **14** Now it was a Sabbath day when Jesus made the mud and opened his eyes. **15** So the Pharisees again asked him how he had received his sight. And he said to them, "He put mud on my eyes, and I washed, and I see." **16** Some of the Pharisees said, "This man is not from God, for he does not keep the Sabbath." But others said, "How can a man who is a sinner do such signs?" And there was a division among them. **17** So they said again to the blind man, "What do you say about him, since he has opened your eyes?" He said, "He is a prophet."

18 The Jews did not believe that he had been blind and had received his sight, until they called the parents of the man who had received his sight **19** and asked them, "Is this your son, who you say was born blind? How then does he now see?" **20** His parents answered, "We know that this is our son and that he was born blind. **21** But how he now sees we do not know, nor do we know who opened his eyes. Ask him; he is of age. He will speak for himself." **22** (His parents said these things because they feared the Jews, for the Jews had already agreed that if anyone should confess Jesus to be Christ, he was to be put out of the synagogue.) **23** Therefore his parents said, "He is of age; ask him."

24 So for the second time they called the man who had been blind and said to him, "Give glory to God. We know that this man is a sinner." **25** He answered, "Whether he is a sinner I do not know. One thing I do know,

that though I was blind, now I see." **26** They said to him, "What did he do
to you? How did he open your eyes?" **27** He answered them, "I have told
you already, and you would not listen. Why do you want to hear it again?
Do you also want to become his disciples?" **28** And they reviled him, saying, "You are his disciple, but we are disciples of Moses. **29** We know that
God has spoken to Moses, but as for this man, we do not know where he
comes from." **30** The man answered, "Why, this is an amazing thing!
You do not know where he comes from, and yet he opened my eyes.
31 We know that God does not listen to sinners, but if anyone is a worshiper
of God and does his will, God listens to him. **32** Never since the world began
has it been heard that anyone opened the eyes of a man born blind. **33** If this
man were not from God, he could do nothing." **34** They answered him, "You
were born in utter sin, and would you teach us?" And they cast him out.

35 Jesus heard that they had cast him out, and having found him he said, "Do
you believe in the Son of Man?" **36** He answered, "And who is he, sir, that I
may believe in him?" **37** Jesus said to him, "You have seen him, and it is he
who is speaking to you." **38** He said, "Lord, I believe," and he worshiped him.
39 Jesus said, "For judgment I came into this world, that those who do not
see may see, and those who see may become blind." **40** Some of the Pharisees
near him heard these things, and said to him, "Are we also blind?" **41** Jesus
said to them, "If you were blind, you would have no guilt; but now that you
say, 'We see,' your guilt remains."

Write down your insights. What stands out to you initially? Also, note any questions you have while reading the text.

Determine Context

Read John 8:58–59. The immediate context of the verses before the blind man was healed shows us that Jesus was escaping a crowd of Jews ready to stone Him. While leaving the temple, we meet Jesus as He passed by a man who was blind from birth. Jesus' disciples, who were following common Jewish thought of the day, assumed that the man's blindness was caused directly by the sin of the man or his parents. Jesus corrected this false way of thinking in verse 3.

Why was this correction necessary for the disciples to know as His representatives? Why is it essential for us to know today?

A particularly important element in this miracle story is that it took place on **the Sabbath**. The Sabbath was a weekly day of rest put in place by God for the benefit of His people. The Sabbath is modeled after God's act of rest on the seventh day of creation (Gen. 2:2–3).

In Exodus, we also see God instructing the Israelites to prepare their food in advance so that they would not have to work for their meals on their day of rest (Ex. 16:22–23). Even if you don't cook, you can probably imagine that making a solid meal requires a lot of preparation and work, especially in the first century! If a Jewish family in Jesus' day wanted something as simple as fresh bread, the women were tasked with the skilled work of preparing everything. Baking a fresh loaf required manual labor over the dough, mixing and kneading it by hand until it was perfect.

The Sabbath refers to a weekly day of rest put in place by God, for the benefit of His people, and modeled after His own act of rest on the seventh day of creation.

To make mud, Jesus had to, in a sense, knead dirt and saliva. He used His spit and mud from the ground and created a paste to put over the blind man's eyes. The concept of kneading or creating this paste was important to the Pharisees because it did constitute work. Therefore, it is an ironically significant element in this miracle story of the blind man. As we learned when discussing Nicodemus in Week 3, the Pharisees adhered strictly to the law. One of the laws they cared intensely about protecting was the Sabbath. So, things get tricky in how the Pharisees choose to interpret the idea of kneading in relation to how Jesus heals the blind man. John Piper puts the controversy plainly:

> [Jesus] used mud because he knew it was Saturday, the Sabbath, and it's against the law to knead dough or clay or mud. One of the 39 interpretations of the Pharisees as to what it means not to work on Saturday was you can't knead dough. And the word for "dough" is identical (pēlon) to the word "mud" or "clay." . . . [Jesus] knew exactly what he was doing. "I'm going to break the law" . . . the law as the Pharisees understood it. Why would he want to do that? Because he's the Lord of the Sabbath, and he wants to show that he is—or to show what the point of the Sabbath is: rest. Why? Why do you need rest? Healing.[23]

Jesus Himself is rest. Jesus Himself is life. Jesus Himself is the standard for perfect living on the Sabbath or any other day. So, He brought true rest and healing to the blind man on the Sabbath! Jesus was intentional about healing this man with mud to show the Pharisees that He was Lord over all. But the Pharisees couldn't let go of their standards of right and wrong and how the law should be interpreted. Despite seeing Jesus perform this miracle, the Pharisees stayed stubbornly fixated on resisting Him, letting the fear of losing power drive them to shut Him out.

This led them unable to comprehend a world in which they were challenged, even by God Himself. So, when the blind man left Jesus with sight, the Pharisees left Jesus still blind.

None of us would like to think we may be similar to the Pharisees in any way. But step back and take an honest look at your life and your faith. Are there any areas where you may be adding to God's Word and then judging others for not following the additional standards you've put into place?

The theme of belief continues in chapter 9 as Jesus asks the now-seeing blind man, "Do you believe in the Son of Man?" (v. 35). Look at the man's response in verse 38.

Reflect

The blind man has two responses: faith and worship. His entire life has changed for the better, and these reactions make perfect sense! But what about when our lives take a difficult turn, and we encounter situations that don't make sense? Can we still have faith and worship? Reflect on where your heart is this week and how you can still practice these two responses to Jesus no matter what you face.

WEEK 5 | DAY 2

To See Jesus or Stay Blind

Assess the Main Idea

Now that we have become familiar with John 9:1–41, our goal is to assess the main idea and figure out what this passage means.

Annotate

Reread John 9:1–41, but this time focus on some key components of the passage, such as:

Highlight the names of **Jesus** and **God** **in purple**:

- Rabbi, the Light of the world, prophet, Christ, Son of Man, God

Highlight the following **character references** **in green**:

- A man blind from birth, parents (of blind man), Pharisees

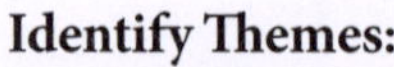

Identify Themes:

- Circle theme of **blindness** **in blue**:
  - Blind
- Circle themes of **sight** **in red**:
  - Sight, see, seeing, sees, seen
- Highlight any formats of **belief** **in yellow**:
  - Believe

Taylor's Annotation Example: **John 9:1–41**

1 As he passed by, he saw a man blind from birth. **2** And his
disciples asked him, "Rabbi, who sinned, this man or his parents,
that he was born blind?" **3** Jesus answered, "It was not that this
man sinned, or his parents, but that the works of God might be
displayed in him. **4** We must work the works of him who sent
me while it is day; night is coming, when no one can work. **5** As
long as I am in the world, I am the light of the world." **6** Having
said these things, he spit on the ground and made mud with the
saliva. Then he anointed the man's eyes with the mud **7** and said
to him, "Go, wash in the pool of Siloam" (which means Sent). So
he went and washed and came back seeing.

Jesus corrects the disciples' incorrect logic. This is important because His earthly ministry is not going to last much longer; He is training the disciples to be His representatives, and to have their minds renewed to think rightly, and to represent him well.

8 The neighbors and those who had seen him before as a beggar were saying, "Is this not the man who used to sit and beg?"
9 Some said, "It is he." Others said, "No, but he is like him." He
kept saying, "I am the man." **10** So they said to him, "Then how
were your eyes opened?" **11** He answered, "The man called Jesus
made mud and anointed my eyes and said to me, 'Go to Siloam
and wash.' So I went and washed and received my sight." **12** They
said to him, "Where is he?" He said, "I do not know."

13 They brought to the Pharisees the man who had formerly

been blind. **14** Now it was a Sabbath day when Jesus made the
mud and opened his eyes. **15** So the Pharisees again asked
him how he had received his sight. And he said to them, "He
put mud on my eyes, and I washed, and I see." **16** Some of the
Pharisees said, "This man is not from God, for he does not keep
the Sabbath." But others said, "How can a man who is a sinner
do such signs?" And there was a division among them. **17** So
they said again to the blind man, "What do you say about him,
since he has opened your eyes?" He said, "He is a prophet."

The Sabbath was a weekly day of rest, put in place by God for the benefit of His people.

18 The Jews did not believe that he had been blind and had received his sight, until they called the parents of the man who had
received his sight **19** and asked them, "Is this your son, who you
say was born blind? How then does he now see?" **20** His parents
answered, "We know that this is our son and that he was born
blind. **21** But how he now sees we do not know, nor do we know
who opened his eyes. Ask him; he is of age. He will speak for
himself." **22** (His parents said these things because they feared
the Jews, for the Jews had already agreed that if anyone should
confess Jesus to be Christ, he was to be put out of the synagogue.)
23 Therefore his parents said, "He is of age; ask him."

The synagogue was an extremely important place for a Jewish person. That is not only where they gathered to study God's Word, but it also functioned as the main center for community. This was where everybody built their relationships, shaped their faith, and connected over their culture. To be removed from this would be devastating and isolating.

24 So for the second time they called the man who had been
blind and said to him, "Give glory to God. We know that this

man is a sinner." **25** He answered, "Whether he is a sinner I do
not know. One thing I do know, that though I was blind, now
I see." **26** They said to him, "What did he do to you? How did
he open your eyes?" **27** He answered them, "I have told you
already, and you would not listen. Why do you want to hear
it again? Do you also want to become his disciples?" **28** And
they reviled him, saying, "You are his disciple, but we are disciples of Moses. **29** We know that God has spoken to Moses,
but as for this man, we do not know where he comes from."
30 The man answered, "Why, this is an amazing thing! You do
not know where he comes from, and yet he opened my eyes.
31 We know that God does not listen to sinners, but if anyone is a
worshiper of God and does his will, God listens to him. **32** Never
since the world began has it been heard that anyone opened the
eyes of a man born blind. **33** If this man were not from God, he
could do nothing." **34** They answered him, "You were born in
utter sin, and would you teach us?" And they cast him out.

35 Jesus heard that they had cast him out, and having found him
he said, "Do you believe in the Son of Man?" **36** He answered,
"And who is he, sir, that I may believe in him?" **37** Jesus said to
him, "You have seen him, and it is he who is speaking to you."
38 He said, "Lord, I believe," and he worshiped him. **39** Jesus

said, "For judgment I came into this world, that those who do
not see may see, and those who see may become blind." **40** Some
of the Pharisees near him heard these things, and said to him,
"Are we also blind?" **41** Jesus said to them, "If you were blind,
you would have no guilt; but now that you say, 'We see,' your
guilt remains."

Paraphrase

John 9:1–41 is split into six sections for paraphrasing. The first three summaries will be filled out for you to read and reflect on, and you can finish the last three on your own. Try to keep your summaries around two sentences. You can look back at the passage for help.

John 9:1–7:

Jesus heals a blind man by putting mud on his eyes and having him wash it off in the pool of Siloam. The man's blindness is so the glory of God might be displayed in Him, not because the man sinned.

John 9:8–12:

When the blind man is asked how his eyes were opened, he claims it was from, "The man called Jesus."

John 9:13–17:

The blind man is brought to the Pharisees who argue that Jesus is not from God because He does not keep the Sabbath. When they ask the blind man who he believes Jesus is, he claims, "He is a prophet."

John 9:18–23:

John 9:24–34:

John 9:35–41:

Main Idea

So, what's the main point of this passage? Jesus is the only one who can give us spiritual sight. For all of us who humbly long to embrace Christ as King, He will open our eyes. But those, like the Pharisees, who refuse Christ will be unable to see Him for who He is and will not experience the salvation and freedom that only come through Him.

Reflect

Describe a time when God opened your eyes to His truth in an area of your life where you were previously "blind." Why were you previously unable to see His way, and how did realizing the truth humble you?

WEEK 5 | DAY 3

What Do You Say?

Seek God and His Character

It's time to dive deep into who God is in this passage. In John 9, the Pharisees claim to *know* who God is when they actually don't. They think they can see when they are really spiritually blind. The Pharisees are like many today who wrestle with resistance to God. But when any of us choose not to embrace God's true character, as the Pharisees did, we will feel lost and disconnected from the source of life.

Reflect

Reread John 9:1–41 and take time to **reflect** on the true character of Jesus. Write down two characteristics of Jesus that stand out to you. They can be implied from the text or explicitly stated. I will start you off with an example.

Taylor's Example

Jesus is the Light of the world (v. 5).
Why does this characteristic stand out to you?

Whether I am dealing with mental health battles that bring lingering darkness or I see the brokenness of the world leaving many without hope, I know that Light has come, and Christ will come again to make all things new. Jesus gives me the hope to push forward with strength. The darkness I face isn't a sign that light doesn't exist, but a reason to seek Christ and His renewing and healing love.

Jesus is ______________________ (v.________).

Why does this characteristic stand out to you?

____

____

____

____

Jesus is ______________________ (v.________).

Why does this characteristic stand out to you?

____

____

____

____

Read

Read John 9:13–17. The Pharisees avoid acknowledging what a miracle the healing of the blind man is because they are focused on questioning Jesus' character. They pressure the blind man for his opinion of Jesus, asking him, "What do you say about him, since he has opened your eyes?" (v. 17). While it is unlikely that they are genuinely seeking to know the truth, their question is still striking with enduring relevance to us today.

Many people in modern society are asking the same questions of us: *What makes you believe in Jesus? Why Christianity? How can you trust that Jesus is the only way?*

Reflect

Thinking about your journey of knowing Jesus, what would you say to the skeptic asking you about His character? Take time to answer the Pharisees' question, "What do you say about him?"

Prayer

Jesus came to be the Light in a dark world, displaying His power and giving hope to those who are humble. He gets all the glory for giving us spiritual sight and salvation. On the lines below, take time to thank God for who He is and how He has saved you.

"What do *you say* about Him?"

Different ways to talk about Jesus

TO THE HURTING:
Jesus draws near to us in our pain and brokenness. He is mighty to save us in our lowest state. You don't have to fear Him leaving.
Psalm 34:18

TO THE SEEKER:
Jesus came to this world to reveal Himself to you and to redeem you to Himself. He is the image of the invisible God making knowing Him possible.
Colossians 1:13–16

TO THE LOST:
Jesus is the one who pursues us, gives us a new story, and offers a life full of purpose. He willingly took our sins upon Himself to bring us back home to Him.
Isaiah 53:6

TO THE THINKER:
The Word was with God and was God since the beginning. Therefore, Jesus isn't just a religious figure—He's the eternal reason, logic, and source behind all that exists.
John 1:1

TO THE NONCONFORMIST:
It is for freedom that Christ has come to set us free. He lived perfectly for us—we don't have to have the burden to save ourselves. We can be free from the baggage of sin that enslaved us.
Galatians 5:1

WEEK 5 | DAY 4

Responding to Jesus

Yearn for a Heart Change and Deeper Intimacy with God

To close out this week's study of John 9:1–41, you will reflect and apply the passage to your life. Often in Scripture, your emotions will be stirred by the actions of people, and this is the perfect time for self-reflection. Today, you will connect with the individuals found in this passage.

We observed many personality dynamics among the people in the story. First, there are the parents of the blind man who let the fear of what other people thought keep them from standing up for what they knew to be true. Then there are the Pharisees, who stubbornly dug their heels in to hold on to their control and "truth." Finally, there is the blind man and his journey to believing. Through it all, he stood up for the facts, risked looking crazy, and ultimately humbled himself to accept Christ.

Read

Take time to read John 9:18–41. As you read, focus on the parents' **fear**, the Pharisees' **pride**, and the blind man's **faith**.

Have you felt afraid of what people will think of you if you openly associate yourself with Christ? Have you ever struggled to believe God's Word because you didn't know if you could trust it? Have you ever been filled with so much excitement about your faith that you couldn't help but worship?

Each of these individuals experienced a very different response to Jesus, and yet we can look within ourselves and relate to each of them. For today's yearning for a heart change, you are going to have an opportunity to learn from each of these people and reflect on how you want to live your life differently because of them. There will be three action steps for you to walk through. You may not be able to do all of them right now but ask the Holy Spirit to guide you on when to implement each one.

Action for Combating Fear

The parents of the blind man let fear keep them from proclaiming Jesus' name. They knew that associating themselves with Jesus would cost them their reputation. They wouldn't be taken seriously and would be kicked out of their religious circle.

Take time to assess your heart honestly. When do you struggle to associate yourself with Jesus? Is it at work? Or within certain friend groups? Maybe it's in your academic pursuits? What costs do you count when it comes to sharing your faith with others?

What would your daily life look like if you confidently embraced your identity as a Christ follower? What steps can you take to challenge yourself to live in that boldness, even if it means sacrificing the promotion at work, your invitation to the party, or respect from your teachers and peers?

Action for Combating Pride

The Pharisees rejected Jesus because of their pride. But pride isn't unique to the Pharisees. We can find it in every human heart. Pride convinces us we know best and don't need to depend on God's Word. It makes us the center of our lives and tells us to live however we want.

Like the Pharisees, pride can prevent us from believing what God has revealed to be true in His Word. Scripture challenges us to set aside our preconceived notions about God and life and be open to renewing our minds. This means challenging our thoughts about God, who we are in Christ, and how we should live.

Take some time in prayer to ask God where pride is keeping you from embracing His truth. Find a few verses of Scripture you want to encourage your heart to believe. This might look like asking God to help you believe the truth about His character, rather than lies, by identifying verses that remind you that He is a loving, present, and forgiving Father. Or, this may involve challenging your negative beliefs about yourself and choosing to focus on the truth by finding Scripture passages that remind you that you are loved, chosen, wonderfully made, and wanted. It might also look like humbling yourself to see how God wants you to live your life and focusing on passages about dying to self, loving your enemies, forgiving those who have hurt you, and denying the pull of what culture says matters.

Find a Scripture verse that applies to an area you are battling pride in, and write it down below. Spend time praying through it.

Action for Bold Worship

The blind man accepted Christ and immediately began to worship. This is easy to do when we first come to faith and are filled with a radical sense of excitement. As time goes on, we can take our faith for granted. We fall out of routines and forget to get back on track. We prioritize our personal lives over spending time with God.

Challenge yourself to make room for ten minutes of dedicated time to worship God today. Your worship can be expressed in many ways. If you are creative, you can invite God into music by singing worship songs, playing instruments, or composing music or lyrics. You can express it through art by painting, collaging, or drawing for God's glory. You can go on a prayer walk, talking to God and praising Him for who He is and for His creation. You can write a heartfelt prayer to God and pray on your knees. Find something that speaks to you, and enjoy your one-on-one time with God.

WEEK 5 | DAY 5

Committing to Memory

Dig Deeper

DIG DEEPER

Yesterday, you chose a Scripture verse to pray through to combat pride. Memorizing verses that challenge and encourage you is a great way to go beyond a one-time prayer to dig deeper into Scripture. Committing the Bible to memory is a form of worship and meditation, as you glorify God in your dedication to His Word and fill your mind with truth to meditate on. Today, you will dig deeper into the verse you chose by memorizing it using the one-letter method.

In this memorization method, you take the first letter of every word and write it down in place of the full word. Doing so helps your brain create a shortcut to recall the verse without leaving you dependent on every word. It forces you to build muscle memory to remember the words without giving everything away. And it helps speed up the time it takes to memorize.

Here is an example of how I use the one-letter method to memorize. The area of pride I want to combat is a lack of trust in God. In good times, it's easy to believe He is on my side, but when things get hard, I tend to question His faithfulness and control. I want to challenge my brain to believe He will be faithful to me in hard times by memorizing Psalm 23:4, which says:

> Even though I walk through the valley of the shadow of death,
> I will fear no evil,
> for you are with me;
> your rod and your staff,
> they comfort me.

With the one-letter method, I take each of the first letters of the words and write them down to look at. Each letter reminds me of the full word without me relying on seeing the full text. Psalm 23:4:

ETIWTTVOTSOD,
IWFNE,
FYAWM;
YRAYS,
TCM.

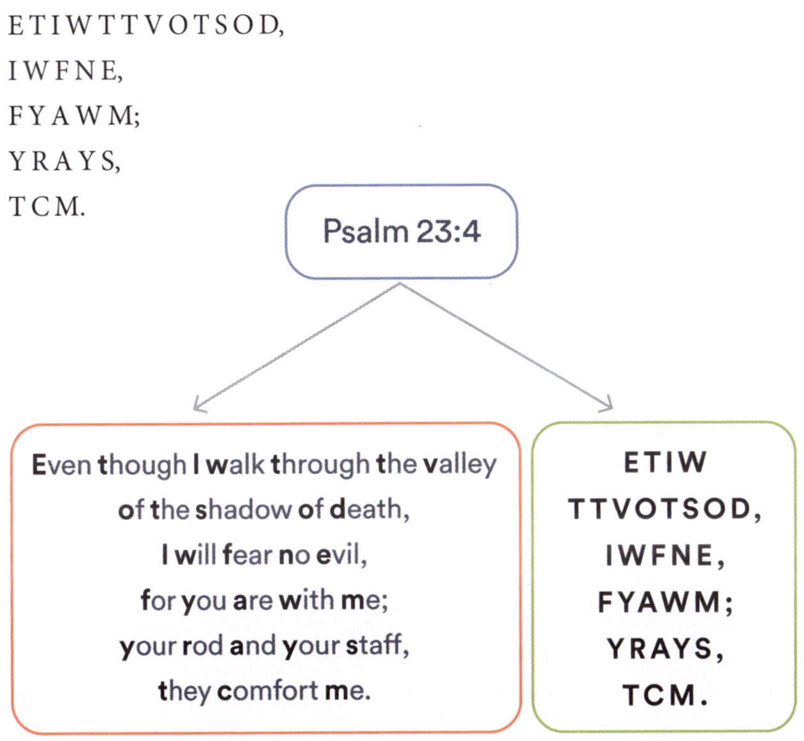

Now, I will give you space to rewrite the verse you want to memorize, followed by the first letter of each word.

Full verse:

One-letter method:

To help you continue your journey in memorizing your verses, have your one-letter method written out somewhere you look often. This can be displayed on your phone's wallpaper, a piece of paper on your desk, or a sticky note attached to your mirror or car dashboard. The one-letter method works great for temporary passwords as well, particularly for smaller verses. Every time you need to unlock your device, you type in your verse as the password until you have it memorized. Then, you can move on to a new verse to memorize. You will be surprised at how quickly your brain will memorize Scripture when you consistently read and meditate on it!

The Journey Continues

The blind man's eyes were transformed by Jesus' miracle-working power, and he was able to see the face of the Messiah. Through the story of his healing, we learned that Jesus alone can open our eyes to see God, and He is worthy of our trust. By believing in Him, we have the spiritual sight we need. As we grow in our relationship with Him, we can combat any Pharisee-like pride that keeps us from putting our faith in Him and fight the fear that hinders us from proclaiming His name.

Next week, we will witness one of Christ's last miracles before He made His way to the cross. Jesus raised Lazarus from the dead, showing His divine power. And Lazarus wasn't the only person Jesus raised. We'll also discover that He was ready to be the resurrection and life for all who believe.

Discussion Questions

To help you reflect on the week of study, here are optional discussion questions that you can discuss with a friend, mentor, or small group.

1. Which person did you connect with most while reading? Why?
2. Jesus points out that the man's blindness was not caused by sin. Why is this important for us to know today?
3. What does John 9:39 mean in the context of this passage, as well as for us today?
4. The blind man's parents were motivated by fear. Are there any specific ways that fear has kept you from living fully for Christ?
5. The blind man's belief in Jesus caused him to worship Him immediately. What are one or two ways God is moving you to worship Him in your daily life?

WEEK 6

Raised to Life

John 11:1–44

By Taylor

It was the summer before sixth grade that my grandma was diagnosed with a brain tumor on Mother's Day. My world was rocked as I watched her decline rapidly.

In the stillness of the room where she lay, we played hymns on her CD player. She was a woman of faith, and we hoped she could hear the worship music as she prepared to meet Jesus.

In her final moments, we experienced a gloriously unexpected moment from God. After days of being unconscious, she suddenly opened her eyes, lifted her face to the heavens, and radiated the biggest smile I'd seen in months.

The world stood still as we savored this message of hope. She passed away shortly after, but the room was filled with peace. My grandma knew where she was going and the Savior who paid the price to get her there.

This week, we are reading about the last miracle Jesus performed before He went to the cross. It involved a man named Lazarus who approached death, and his family who called frantically for Jesus to heal Him. But Jesus had greater plans.

WEEK 6 | DAY 1

See How He Loved

Enter into the Story

Prayer

Start your Bible study time with this prayer. Quiet your heart, slow down, and read each word out loud to the Lord:

Dear Lord, thank You for the time I get to read Your Word. I proclaim over my soul that You are the resurrection and the life. I believe in You and Your power to save. Be glorified in my time of study. Amen.

Read slowly and thoughtfully

Open your Bible to John 11:1–44. Read it slowly and thoughtfully. The passage is also included for you here.

Listen to the text while reading

John 11:1–44

The Death of Lazarus

1 Now a certain man was ill, Lazarus of Bethany, the village of Mary and her
sister Martha. **2** It was Mary who anointed the Lord with ointment and wiped
his feet with her hair, whose brother Lazarus was ill. **3** So the sisters sent to
him, saying, "Lord, he whom you love is ill." **4** But when Jesus heard it he said,
"This illness does not lead to death. It is for the glory of God, so that the Son
of God may be glorified through it."

5 Now Jesus loved Martha and her sister and Lazarus. **6** So, when he heard
that Lazarus was ill, he stayed two days longer in the place where he was.
7 Then after this he said to the disciples, "Let us go to Judea again." **8** The
disciples said to him, "Rabbi, the Jews were just now seeking to stone you,
and are you going there again?" **9** Jesus answered, "Are there not twelve
hours in the day? If anyone walks in the day, he does not stumble, because he
sees the light of this world. **10** But if anyone walks in the night, he stumbles,
because the light is not in him." **11** After saying these things, he said to
them, "Our friend Lazarus has fallen asleep, but I go to awaken him." **12** The
disciples said to him, "Lord, if he has fallen asleep, he will recover." **13** Now Jesus
had spoken of his death, but they thought that he meant taking rest in sleep.
14 Then Jesus told them plainly, "Lazarus has died, **15** and for your sake I am
glad that I was not there, so that you may believe. But let us go to him." **16** So
Thomas, called the Twin, said to his fellow disciples, "Let us also go, that we
may die with him."

I Am the Resurrection and the Life

17 Now when Jesus came, he found that Lazarus had already been in the
tomb four days. **18** Bethany was near Jerusalem, about two miles off, **19** and
many of the Jews had come to Martha and Mary to console them concerning
their brother. **20** So when Martha heard that Jesus was coming, she went and
met him, but Mary remained seated in the house. **21** Martha said to Jesus,
"Lord, if you had been here, my brother would not have died. **22** But even
now I know that whatever you ask from God, God will give you." **23** Jesus
said to her, "Your brother will rise again." **24** Martha said to him, "I know that
he will rise again in the resurrection on the last day." **25** Jesus said to her, "I
am the resurrection and the life. Whoever believes in me, though he die, yet
shall he live, **26** and everyone who lives and believes in me shall never die.
Do you believe this?" **27** She said to him, "Yes, Lord; I believe that you are the
Christ, the Son of God, who is coming into the world."

Jesus Weeps

28 When she had said this, she went and called her sister Mary, saying in
private, "The Teacher is here and is calling for you." **29** And when she heard
it, she rose quickly and went to him. **30** Now Jesus had not yet come into the
village, but was still in the place where Martha had met him. **31** When the
Jews who were with her in the house, consoling her, saw Mary rise quickly
and go out, they followed her, supposing that she was going to the tomb to
weep there. **32** Now when Mary came to where Jesus was and saw him, she
fell at his feet, saying to him, "Lord, if you had been here, my brother would
not have died." **33** When Jesus saw her weeping, and the Jews who had come
with her also weeping, he was deeply moved in his spirit and greatly troubled.
34 And he said, "Where have you laid him?" They said to him, "Lord, come
and see." **35** Jesus wept. **36** So the Jews said, "See how he loved him!" **37** But
some of them said, "Could not he who opened the eyes of the blind man also
have kept this man from dying?"

Jesus Raises Lazarus

38 Then Jesus, deeply moved again, came to the tomb. It was a cave, and a
stone lay against it. **39** Jesus said, "Take away the stone." Martha, the sister of
the dead man, said to him, "Lord, by this time there will be an odor, for he
has been dead four days." **40** Jesus said to her, "Did I not tell you that if you
believed you would see the glory of God?" **41** So they took away the stone.
And Jesus lifted up his eyes and said, "Father, I thank you that you have heard
me. **42** I knew that you always hear me, but I said this on account of the
people standing around, that they may believe that you sent me." **43** When
he had said these things, he cried out with a loud voice, "Lazarus, come out."
44 The man who had died came out, his hands and feet bound with linen
strips, and his face wrapped with a cloth. Jesus said to them, "Unbind him,
and let him go."

Annotate

We are going to be doing a little bit of annotating in Day 1 this week. Start your study of this passage by simply circling:

- The word **love/loved** (3x) **in pink**

Next, write down what stands out to you and any questions you have while reading the text:

Determine Context

While reading this chapter, we meet three of Jesus' friends: Lazarus, Mary, and Martha. This passage is filled with raw emotion as Jesus navigates how He wants to display His glory through Lazarus' life, death, and ultimate resurrection. Not everything goes as Mary and Martha plan, but it is all divinely intentional.

John emphasizes many themes throughout this passage, including Jesus' love. Two of the statements of Jesus' love are placed at the very beginning of this passage, within verses 1–5. These statements set us up to see from the start of this passage that Jesus is motivated by what lies at the very core of Him: love. This is particularly true in how He interacts with people.

We can learn a lot about the loving relationship Jesus forms with Mary in other passages of Scripture. For example, in verse 2, the author John mentions briefly a story of Mary and Jesus that he expects the reader to be familiar with. It can be found in **John 12:1–8**. Take time to read this story and write down what strikes you about Mary's close relationship with Jesus.

The Bible offers more valuable context about Jesus' love for Lazarus by having us consider what Jesus would risk in coming to Judea to rescue Lazarus. When Jesus told His disciples it was time to go back into Judea in verse 7, the disciples responded sharply with confusion that Jesus would willingly go back to such a deadly place.

Take a moment to read **John 10:24–39** to grasp the hostility that Jesus and His disciples would be walking into if they were to return to Lazarus.

John 10:24–39

24 The people surrounded him and asked, "How long are you going to keep us in suspense? If you are the Messiah, tell us plainly."

25 Jesus replied, "I have already told you, and you don't believe me. The proof is the work I do in my Father's name. **26** But you don't believe me because you are not my sheep. **27** My sheep listen to my voice; I know them, and they follow me. **28** I give them eternal life, and they will never perish. No one can snatch them away from me, **29** for my Father has given them to me, and he is more powerful than anyone else. No one can snatch them from the Father's hand. **30** The Father and I are one."

31 Once again the people picked up stones to kill him. 32 Jesus said, "At my Father's direction I have done many good works. For which one are you going to stone me?"

33 They replied, "We're stoning you not for any good work, but for blasphemy! You, a mere man, claim to be God."

34 Jesus replied, "It is written in your own Scriptures that God said to certain leaders of the people, 'I say, you are gods!' **35** And you know that the Scriptures cannot be altered. So if those people who received God's message were called 'gods,' **36** why do you call it blasphemy when I say, 'I am the Son of God'? After all, the Father set me apart and sent me into the world. **37** Don't believe me unless I carry out my Father's work. **38** But if I do his work, believe in the evidence of the miraculous works I have done, even if you don't believe me. Then you will know and understand that the Father is in me, and I am in the Father."

39 Once again they tried to arrest him, but he got away and left them. (NLT emphasis added)

Having read this passage, how does it illustrate for you more vividly the love that Jesus has for Lazarus and his sisters in returning to Judea?

As you close today's study, pray and thank God for His love for you. The story of Lazarus is just a small picture of what Jesus is willing to do for those He loves. He also voluntarily endured death on the cross to bring you close to Him.

WEEK 6 | DAY 2

I Am the Resurrection

Assess the Main Idea

Now that we have become familiar with John 11:1–53, our goal is to assess its main idea and figure out what this passage means.

When it comes to John, we know that his main goal was to help people believe. So, when Jesus presented the heart of the gospel in this chapter (vv. 25–27), we should take note. The time of His earthly ministry was coming close to its end, and He was making it clear that He was the true resurrection and life for all those who believed in Him. The miracle Jesus did for Lazarus pointed to something greater—the future death and resurrection of Christ and the reality that we can all be raised like Lazarus because of Jesus.

Annotate

Annotate **John 11:1–44** to identify key components and themes, such as:

Highlight the name **Jesus** and the other **names of Jesus** in purple:

- Rabbi, Lord, Son of God, resurrection and the life, the Christ, the teacher

Highlight the following **character references** in green:

- Lazarus, Mary, Martha, disciples, Jews

Identify Themes:

- Circle themes of **God's glory** in red:
  - Glory, glorified
- Circle themes of **Jesus' humanity** (seen in His emotions) **in blue**:
  - Deeply moved, greatly troubled, Jesus wept
- Underline the **heart of the gospel** in orange
  - John 11:25–27
- Highlight any formats of **belief** in yellow:
  - Believe, believes, believed

Taylor's Annotation Example: **John 11:1–44**

The Death of Lazarus

1 Now a certain man was ill, Lazarus of Bethany, the village
of Mary and her sister Martha. **2** It was Mary who anointed
the Lord with ointment and wiped his feet with her hair, whose
brother Lazarus was ill. **3** So the sisters sent to him, saying,
"Lord, he whom you love is ill." **4** But when Jesus heard it he
said, "This illness does not lead to death. It is for the glory of
God, so that the Son of God may be glorified through it."

Jesus was motivated in everything He did to glorify God. To glorify God is to reflect His greatness, making much of Him, through our thoughts, words, and deeds.

5 Now Jesus loved Martha and her sister and Lazarus. **6** So,
when he heard that Lazarus was ill, he stayed two days longer in
the place where he was. **7** Then after this he said to the disciples,
"Let us go to Judea again." **8** The disciples said to him, "Rabbi,
the Jews were just now seeking to stone you, and are you going

there again?" **9** Jesus answered, "Are there not twelve hours
in the day? If anyone walks in the day, he does not stumble,
because he sees the light of this world. **10** But if anyone walks
in the night, he stumbles, because the light is not in him."
11 After saying these things, he said to them, "Our friend
Lazarus has fallen asleep, but I go to awaken him." **12** The
disciples said to him, "Lord, if he has fallen asleep, he will
recover." **13** Now Jesus had spoken of his death, but they
thought that he meant taking rest in sleep. **14** Then Jesus told
them plainly, "Lazarus has died, **15** and for your sake I am glad
that I was not there, so that you may believe. But let us go to
him." **16** So Thomas, called the Twin, said to his fellow disciples,
"Let us also go, that we may die with him."

I Am the Resurrection and the Life

17 Now when Jesus came, he found that Lazarus had already
been in the tomb four days. **18** Bethany was near Jerusalem,
about two miles off, **19** and many of the Jews had come to
Martha and Mary to console them concerning their brother.
20 So when Martha heard that Jesus was coming, she went and
met him, but Mary remained seated in the house. **21** Martha
said to Jesus, "Lord, if you had been here, my brother would not
have died. **22** But even now I know that whatever you ask from

God, God will give you." **23** Jesus said to her, "Your brother will
rise again." **24** Martha said to him, "I know that he will rise again
in the resurrection on the last day." **25** Jesus said to her, "I am
the resurrection and the life. Whoever believes in me, though
he die, yet shall he live, **26** and everyone who lives and believes
in me shall never die. Do you believe this?" **27** She said to him,
"Yes, Lord; I believe that you are the Christ, the Son of God, who
is coming into the world."

Jesus presents the heart of the gospel in verses 25–27. The gospel refers to the story of Jesus Christ coming into the world to save people from their sins, offering Himself as a sacrifice to bring everlasting life to those who believe.

Jesus Weeps

28 When she had said this, she went and called her sister Mary,
saying in private, "The Teacher is here and is calling for you."
29 And when she heard it, she rose quickly and went to him.
30 Now Jesus had not yet come into the village, but was still
in the place where Martha had met him. **31** When the Jews
who were with her in the house, consoling her, saw Mary rise
quickly and go out, they followed her, supposing that she was
going to the tomb to weep there. **32** Now when Mary came to
where Jesus was and saw him, she fell at his feet, saying to him,
"Lord, if you had been here, my brother would not have died."
33 When Jesus saw her weeping, and the Jews who had come
with her also weeping, he was deeply moved in his spirit and
greatly troubled. **34** And he said, "Where have you laid him?"

They said to him, "Lord, come and see." **35** Jesus wept. **36** So the
Jews said, "See how he loved him!" **37** But some of them said,
"Could not he who opened the eyes of the blind man also have
kept this man from dying?"

Jesus Raises Lazarus

38 Then Jesus, deeply moved again, came to the tomb. It was
a cave, and a stone lay against it. **39** Jesus said, "Take away
the stone." Martha, the sister of the dead man, said to him,
"Lord, by this time there will be an odor, for he has been dead
four days." **40** Jesus said to her, "Did I not tell you that if you
believed you would see the glory of God?" **41** So they took away
the stone. And Jesus lifted up his eyes and said, "Father, I thank
you that you have heard me. **42** I knew that you always hear
me, but I said this on account of the people standing around,
that they may believe that you sent me." **43** When he had said
these things, he cried out with a loud voice, "Lazarus, come out."
44 The man who had died came out, his hands and feet bound
with linen strips, and his face wrapped with a cloth. Jesus said
to them, "Unbind him, and let him go."

There is more than meets the surface with the phrase "deeply moved". Jesus was not just sad about Lazarus being gone, but likely angered at the reality of death.

Paraphrase

I have split John 11:1–53 into six sections for paraphrasing. The first three summaries are already completed for you to read and reflect on. You can finish the last two on your own. Try to keep your summaries between one and two sentences to develop a firmer grasp of the text.

John 11:1–6:

When sisters Mary and Martha send word to Jesus that Lazarus is ill, He delays leaving for two days so that the glory of God would be displayed.

John 11:7–16:

The disciples are confused as to why Jesus wants to go to Judea to awaken Lazarus. So, Jesus explains that Lazarus has died, and His absence will help them believe.

John 11:17–27:

When Jesus asks Martha if she believes that He is the resurrection and the life and that whoever believes in Him will live, she believes and calls Him the Christ, the Son of God.

John 11:28–37:

John 11:38–44:

Reflect

After paraphrasing this chapter, how do verses 25–27 stand out as particularly important? Remember that Jesus intentionally made this one of His last and most dramatic miracles before His own journey to the grave and back.

Main Idea

So, what's the main point of this passage? Jesus is *the* resurrection and life for all who believe in Him!

Finish today by praying through the gospel presented in verses 25–27 and journaling on what it means in your life.

WEEK 6 | DAY 3

He Was Deeply Moved

Seek God and His Character

Jesus' humanity is a central theme in John 11. While He is supremely powerful in raising Lazarus from the dead, He is also deeply in touch with His emotions when facing our brokenness. Jesus shows us that He is both fully God and fully man. We worship a loving, grieving, and present Savior.

Reflect

Take time to reflect on John 11 and the true character of Jesus. Write down three characteristics of Jesus that resonate the most with you. I will start with an example.

Taylor's Example

Jesus is glorious (v. 4).

____________________ (v.______).

____________________ (v.______).

____________________ (v.______).

Read John 11:28–44. This section of the passage is filled with tension and emotion. Mary and the Jews mourning around her are visibly upset at the death of Lazarus. We also catch a small glimpse into the brokenness of the human heart in verse 37: "Could not he who opened the eyes of the blind man also have kept this man from dying?" Jesus sees that those around Him are filled with unbelief.

Consistently throughout His ministry, He has been questioned, mocked, and doubted, and here He faces this painful reality once more.

Jesus is also pained by the loss of a close friend, someone whom He loves deeply. He cries publicly over this, showing His emotions freely. Jesus connects to the humanity of Martha and Mary by demonstrating that He, too, is human—feeling the weight of losing someone close.

As a response to the brokenness that He finds Himself surrounded by, the text tells us that He becomes "deeply moved in his spirit" (v. 33). Scholars have pointed out that this verse shows Jesus is more than sad, but angry; it is best understood as a mixture of anger and grief, with His anger being directed at death.[24] Jesus is indignant at death and the destruction of sin because He knows fully—being God—that this was never His plan for humanity.

Only Jesus can understand what it is like to carry the weight of the world on His shoulders as He dies on the cross. Only Jesus can understand what it is like to take on the full wrath of God. Only Jesus knows what it is like to die for those He knows would never believe in Him.

It is His never-ending love that drives Him to the cross, while His anger at death reveals the holiness of His heart to abhor the evil effects of sin and face our greatest enemy on our behalf. He hates that we would be separated from God the Father so much that He would sacrifice Himself to bring us back to Him.

How are you moved by Christ's emotions in this passage, particularly His anger toward death?

Read James 1:19–21 which shows that human anger is different than God's holy anger.

Human Anger ≠ God's Anger

Human anger is usually corrupted by sin—tainted by pride, selfishness, or a desire to control.	God's anger is holy, perfect, just, and always aimed at sin and evil. It flows out of His love for goodness and justice.

Even if our anger feels righteous, it usually leads to sin (selfish actions, harsh words, bitterness). Our anger can lead us away from love, mercy, humility, and forgiveness.

Think about what you've learned in light of Jesus' response to Lazarus' death. Why is Jesus' anger acceptable while our anger needs warnings and limitations?

Jesus experienced the fullness of what it means to be human. We know He can understand all of our pain. Journal your thankfulness for His emotional availability and human relatability.

Pray

Read Hebrews 4:15–16. As you close, keep these verses in mind, draw near to God with confidence, and write a prayer to Him below.

WEEK 6 | DAY 4

For God's Glory

Yearn for a Heart Change and Deeper Intimacy with God

To close out this week's study of John 11:1–44, you will reflect on and apply this passage to your life. We see several times throughout these verses that Jesus was motivated in everything He did to glorify God. We have witnessed this to be true of Jesus throughout the gospel of John. This also needs to be true for us, as we were created to bring glory to God.

John Piper says that glorifying God means "feeling and thinking and acting in ways that reflect his greatness, that make much of God, that give evidence of the supreme greatness of all his attributes and the all-satisfying beauty of his manifold perfections."[25]

In yearning for a heart change, we want the gospel message to motivate us to reflect God's greatness and make much of Him. We don't simply receive Christ's forgiveness and forget about Him. The gospel should spur us on to live a new life in our resurrection. Even while here on earth, Jesus makes us new.

Reflect

What areas of your life has Christ resurrected that you want to give Him glory for? Think about your testimony: addictions you've overcome, relationships He's restored, ways He's renewed your sense of worth, or healing He's brought to your mental health. Take time to thank Him on the lines below.

Read

Read 1 Corinthians 10:31. What are some specific things in your everyday life that you can do to the glory of God?

Read John 11:25–27. What do you think it would look like to live in the confidence of Jesus' resurrection power right now and not just after death? Because you can—it's available to you! Write down a few ways it could help you stand firm through trials, share about God's goodness, and trust in God's will.

Close today's study by praying about how you can glorify God in the coming days. Invite Him to help you do this.

Glorify God in . . .

Thoughts

Be mindful of the thoughts you let take root. Reading God's Word daily can help renew your mind to think like Christ.

Words

Speak in ways that honor God publicly. Let your speech show the world your love for Him and His love for them.

Deeds

Act in ways that align with God's heart. Before making decisions, big or small, pray that God would guide you to live like Jesus.

WEEK 6 | DAY 5

Doctrine of the Resurrection

Dig Deeper

DIG DEEPER Back in Week 1, we talked about how one great way to dig deeper in your Bible study is to look at a commentary. As a reminder, commentaries are helpful because they are written by scholars who study God's Word meticulously.

For today's Dig Deeper, you will look at Warren Wiersbe's commentary, *Be Alive (John 1–12): Get to Know the Living Savior*, focusing on John 11:17–27. Wiersbe mentions the word *doctrine* several times throughout his commentary. I define *doctrine*, in this context, as a foundational teaching that one believes to be from God.

Doctrine refers to a foundational teaching that one believes to be from God.

Begin your time of study by reading John 11:17–27. When you are done, read through the commentary below, highlighting what stands out.

> Martha was quick to affirm her faith in Jesus Christ (John 11:22), and Jesus responded to that faith by promising her that her brother would rise again. He was thinking of the immediate situation, but she interpreted His words to mean the future resurrection in the last day (Dan. 12:2–3; John 5:28–29) . . .
>
> It is important to note that Jesus did not deny what Martha said about the future resurrection. The resurrection of the human body is a cardinal

doctrine in the orthodox Jewish faith. But in His great "I am" statement, our Lord completely transformed the doctrine of the resurrection and, in so doing, brought great comfort to Martha's heart.

To begin with, He brought the doctrine of the resurrection out of the shadows and into the light. The Old Testament revelation about death and resurrection is not clear or complete; it is, as it were, "in the shadows." In fact, there are some passages in Psalms and Ecclesiastes that almost make one believe that death is the end and there is no hope beyond the grave . . .

By His teaching, His miracles, and His own resurrection, Jesus clearly taught the resurrection of the human body. He has declared once for all that death is real, that there is life after death, and that the body will one day be raised by the power of God.

He transformed this doctrine in a second way: He took it out of a book and put it into a person, Himself. "I am the resurrection and the life" (John 11:25)! . . . When you belong to Him, you have all that you ever will need in life, death, time, or eternity! Wherever He is, God's resurrection power is available now.[26]

Journal below what stood out to you from the commentary:

The Journey Continues

Jesus is *the* resurrection and the life! By raising His friend Lazarus from the dead, Jesus demonstrated His divine power over death. But this power isn't limited to Lazarus! Anyone who believes in Him can be the recipient of this everlasting life. Not only that, but we have a Savior who is also able to relate to every emotion we feel—from grief, anger, and joy—because He is fully human. Our God is mighty but also accessible.

Next week, we will meet Thomas. His struggles with doubt are something we can all relate to. Let's see how Jesus met him where he was and what that means for us.

Discussion Questions

To help you reflect on the week of study, here are optional discussion questions that you can discuss with a friend, mentor, or small group.

1. Were there one or two details of this story that stood out to you as you read this passage?
2. Jesus didn't immediately heal Lazarus. Why was this the case and why is that important for us to know?
3. Has there ever been a time you prayed for Jesus to intervene in a difficult time, but He didn't move as quickly as you hoped?
4. Read John 11:25–27. How can these verses encourage you as you navigate through trials in your daily life?
5. The passage shares that Jesus was moved deeply in His spirit and wept (vv. 33, 35). Why is it significant that God reveals His humanity through His raw emotions?

WEEK 7

Doubt to Devotion

John 20:24–29

By Ashley

For me, doubt has sometimes led me to question whether God is truly there. When I pray and get no immediate answers, I struggle to believe that He really does exist. I've told myself plenty of times that being a Christian would be so much easier if I could just see Jesus and talk with Him face-to-face.

But then He reminds me through His Word that He is gracious toward us when we face doubts, and those of us who believe in Him without seeing Him are truly blessed.

We are nearing the end of our journey of exploring faith-filled stories in the book of John together. Last week, we learned about the incredible miracle of Jesus raising Lazarus from the dead. Now we fast-forward to after the death and resurrection of Jesus.

We will take a peek into the life of one of Jesus' disciples, Thomas, and see how he grappled with some serious emotions of doubt after Jesus' death. Thomas' story is *real* and reminds us that facing doubt as a disciple of Christ is a common experience. Doubt can come like a crashing wave, flipping our world upside down, or a quiet whisper, hidden in the everyday moments of life.

WEEK 7 | DAY 1

The Night of Jesus' Death

Enter into the Story

Prayer

Start your Bible study time with this prayer. Quiet your heart, slow down, and read each word out loud to the Lord:

Dear Lord, You are still full of grace and mercy for me even in my questions and doubts. Fill my heart with belief. Lord, I believe—but help my unbelief. Amen.

Remember in Week 2 when we learned about a few of Jesus' disciples, such as Andrew and Peter? Today, we are introduced to another one of Jesus' twelve disciples: **Thomas.**

Read slowly and thoughtfully

Open your Bible to John 20:24–29. Read it slowly and thoughtfully. The passage is also included for you here.

Listen to the text while reading

John 20:24–29

Jesus and Thomas

24 Now Thomas, one of the twelve, called the Twin, was not with them when
Jesus came. **25** So the other disciples told him, "We have seen the Lord." But

> he said to them, "Unless I see in his hands the mark of the nails, and place my finger into the mark of the nails, and place my hand into his side, I will never believe."
>
> **26** Eight days later, his disciples were inside again, and Thomas was with
> them. Although the doors were locked, Jesus came and stood among them
> and said, "Peace be with you." **27** Then he said to Thomas, "Put your finger
> here, and see my hands; and put out your hand, and place it in my side. Do
> not disbelieve, but believe." **28** Thomas answered him, "My Lord and my
> God!" **29** Jesus said to him, "Have you believed because you have seen me?
> Blessed are those who have not seen and yet have believed."

Write down your insights. What stands out to you initially? Also, note any questions you have while reading the text.

Determine Context

The story of Thomas that we just read is at the end of the book of John after Jesus had already risen from the grave. But **let's rewind** a little bit to see what has happened since Jesus raised Lazarus from the grave—because let me tell you, *a lot* has happened! Take a look at this timeline to help you grasp all that has occurred between John 12 and John 20, which spans about one to two weeks.

Jesus' Last Few Days Timeline

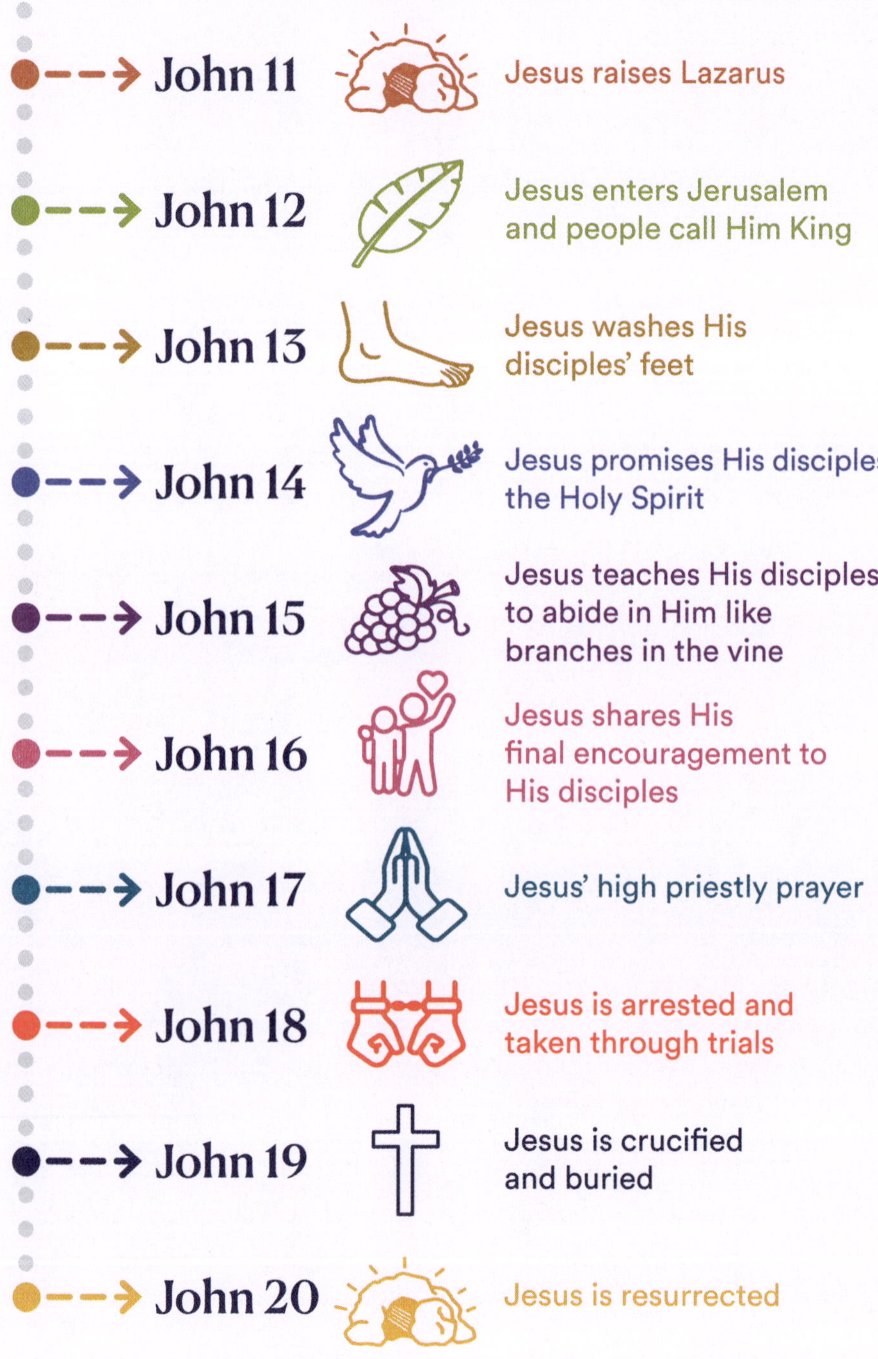

In John 13, Jesus turned His ministry inward to focus on His twelve disciples. Jesus' ministry quickly went from public to private because of the growing hostility and hatred people had toward Him. He knew the time was coming to be crucified—and it was coming very fast.

Jesus focused His last few hours before His arrest on pouring His whole heart into His disciples: washing their feet, sharing the Last Supper, encouraging them, equipping them for the future, and praying for them (John 13–17).

Soon after these intimate moments, one of His beloved disciples, Judas, betrayed Jesus by exposing Him to the authorities, therefore leading Jesus to be arrested. The Jewish authorities handed Jesus over to Pilate, the Roman governor of Judea, so that Pilate could put Him to death. Pilate found Jesus not guilty, so He asked the Jews if Jesus should be released. But the Jews chose Barabbas, a robber, over Jesus to be released (John 18).

Read and Reflect

For around three years, the disciples lived, walked, and breathed Jesus. They grew deep and intimate relationships with Him. They got to know the depths of His heart and felt His unconditional love. They shared hundreds of meals with Him, pouring out their hearts in conversations. They watched Him perform dozens of miracles and transform the lives of many. The disciples wept, laughed, mourned, and rejoiced with Jesus. And these once-ordinary men, whom Jesus had called, *believed* that He was more than just a good man or another prophet. They believed He was the Messiah.

Read John 19 about Jesus' final moments, death, and burial, and put yourself in the shoes of these twelve disciples who had been with Jesus for years. Think about how they may have felt seeing their closest friend and Lord crucified.

Put yourself in the story

Now, turn your thoughts specifically to Thomas. If you were Thomas and saw Jesus crucified after putting your faith in Him and committing your entire life to Him, **what do you imagine he would have been feeling the night of Jesus' death**?

WEEK 7 | DAY 2

Blessed Are Those Who Believe

Assess the Main Idea

Yesterday, you became familiar with Jesus' final days, along with the gruesome death He faced on the cross. But the story doesn't end there. Today, you are going to read about Jesus' resurrection!

Read

Read John 20:1–29. As you read, what main themes stick out to you from the passage?

Annotate

Now, annotate **John 20:24–29**, which focuses on **Jesus and Thomas**, marking some key components of the passage, such as:

Highlight the name **Jesus** and the other **names of Jesus in purple**:

- my Lord, my God

Highlight the following **character references in green**:

- Thomas

Identify **themes:**

- Underline themes of **doubt** in red
- Circle themes of **seeing in blue**
    - See, seen

- Highlight any formats of **belief** in yellow:
    - Believe, believed
- Underline blessed

Ashley's Annotation Example: John 20:24–29

Jesus and Thomas

24 Now Thomas, one of the twelve, called the Twin, was not
with them when Jesus came. **25** So the other disciples told him,
"We have seen the Lord." But he said to them, "Unless I see in
his hands the mark of the nails, and place my finger into the
mark of the nails, and place my hand into his side, I will never
believe."

26 Eight days later, his disciples were inside again, and Thomas
was with them. Although the doors were locked, Jesus came and
stood among them and said, "Peace be with you." **27** Then he
said to Thomas, "Put your finger here, and see my hands; and
put out your hand, and place it in my side. Do not disbelieve,
but believe." **28** Thomas answered him, "My Lord and my God!"
29 Jesus said to him, "Have you believed because you have seen
me? Blessed are those who have not seen and yet have believed."

"Lord" means someone who is in charge. It's the one you belong to—the one who leads you, guides you, and has the final say in your life.

The one true God—the God of Israel.

Inner reward of faith and trust in God:

- deeply joyful
- Spiritually satisfied
- Favored by God

Paraphrase

I have split John 20:24–29 into three sections for paraphrasing. Try to keep your summaries between one to two sentences. You can look back at the passage for help.

John 20:24–25:

John 20:26–28:

John 20:29:

As you can see, the central theme we have been studying throughout the book of John is highlighted here again within Thomas' story: belief versus unbelief.

Many of Thomas' closest friends, the other disciples, had seen Jesus face-to-face, yet Thomas is left to wonder if his friends' words are true. *Had they really seen Jesus?* As Grant Osborne explains, "Thomas's cynicism virtually destroy[s] his faith, for he flatly refuses to believe the witness of his fellow disciples"[27]

For a little over a week, Thomas wrestles with his doubt and skepticism about Jesus' supposed return. But Jesus doesn't leave Thomas there. Instead, **He comes** and offers Himself to Thomas. He meets Thomas at his lowest, in the midst of his doubt and weakness.

Seeing and touching Jesus leads Thomas to declare his belief in Him as his Lord and God (John 20:28). Thomas' transformation is *huge*—he has come to fully affirm that Jesus is truly God! Although it took seeing for Thomas to believe, Jesus shares that those who believe in Him without seeing are truly blessed.

Main Idea

Write out **John 20:29** here, which is the **main point of John's message**.

Reflect

What do you think Jesus means when He says those who believe without seeing are *blessed*? Look up 1 Peter 1:8–9 to help you answer.

I like how Dr. Osborne puts it. He says to be blessed means "God pours out his blessings in a special way on those who find faith even when they have no opportunity to 'see' and walk with Jesus."[28]

Pray

Close today's study time by praying through what you read in 1 Peter 1:8–9.

WEEK 7 | DAY 3

My Lord, My God

 Seek God and His Character

After Jesus revealed Himself to Thomas, Thomas could not help but declare, "My Lord and my God!" (John 20:28). This is powerful and one of the most explicit statements of Jesus' deity, meaning that Thomas is professing Jesus to be God!

Thomas isn't just proclaiming that Jesus is God—he's making it deeply personal: "*My* Lord and *my* God" (John 20:28, emphasis added). It's a wholehearted confession of his relationship with Christ.

Explicit Characteristics of God

Let's look at the two explicit character qualities of Jesus that are mentioned in John 20:28.

Jesus is my Lord.

Jesus is my Lord

"Lord" means someone who has authority and control over a person or thing. He to whom a person or thing belongs. The one who leads, directs, and is in charge.[29]

Reflect

How does Jesus lead your life? In what ways are you inviting Him into every area of your heart? Where do you turn for guidance and direction each day?

Jesus is my God.

Jesus is my God	Specifically in scripture, the Godhead, Trinity, or the one true God, the God of Israel. It is used of Christ, when He is clearly called divine (e.g. John 1:1, John 20:28).[30]

It's a bold and powerful statement to declare that Jesus is God, yet that's exactly what we as Christians do. We believe that Jesus was more than just a good man who walked this earth and more than just a Jewish prophet. We put our hope and faith in that He is God, and He died and rose from the grave to give us eternal life.

Declaring that Jesus is God, as Thomas did, shows that we are combating doubt and embracing faith without seeing. Although we cannot see Jesus with our physical eyes, we believe in Him. We believe not only that He existed historically, but also that He is God and is still alive today.

Here is a chart featuring five verses that directly emphasize that Jesus is God. I filled in the verses and key insights for the first two references in the chart. You can finish the rest. Look up the references and complete the rest of the chart.

Reference:	Verse:	Key Insights
John 1:1	In the beginning was the Word, and the Word was with God, and the Word was God.	Jesus was in the beginning. He was with God the Father and He is God.
John 20:28	Thomas said to him, "My Lord and my God!"	Thomas declares Jesus to be his personal Lord and God.

1 John 5:20		
Romans 9:5		
Titus 2:13		

Prayer

Throughout this study, we have gained a deeper understanding of who Jesus is. Perhaps the greatest character quality we've studied about Him is that **He is God**. If you believe in Jesus as your Lord and Savior and that He is *your* God, declare it to Him right now in a dedicated prayer to Him. If you feel stuck, use these psalms to help guide your prayer: Psalm 18:2, Psalm 31:14, and Psalm 63:1.

WEEK 7 | DAY 4

Facing Doubt Head-On

Yearn for a Heart Change and Deeper Intimacy with God

My favorite movie growing up was *The Polar Express*. Even after I stopped believing in Santa, I continued to watch it every year because of its beautiful theme of childlike faith.

If you haven't seen it, *The Polar Express* is about a boy who's struggling to believe in Santa. One Christmas Eve, a magical train bound for the North Pole arrives at his house. He hesitantly boards it last minute, and the remainder of the film follows his journey of wrestling with doubt and slowly learning to believe in Santa again.

During the boy's journey to the North Pole, he encounters a mysterious hobo multiple times. As they near their destination, the boy sees him again in an abandoned train car filled with old, broken toys. Throughout the film, the hobo represents the boy's inner doubting voice. The hobo picks up a dirty, broken Ebenezer Scrooge puppet and declares in a loud, frightening voice, "You . . . are a DOUBTER! A doubter, you don't believe!"[31] This scene shows us three important things:

1. The intensity of the child's inner doubting voice. It is strong and loud, drowning out the joy of Christmas.
2. The boy cannot escape the doubting voice. The closer he gets to the North Pole, the stronger the hobo's message of doubt becomes.
3. On the journey, the boy struggles with doubt and faces it head-on. He asks questions. He has a healthy amount of skepticism. Ultimately, he chooses to forgo the voice of doubt and believe in Santa even before he can see Santa.

Now, I'm not sharing this to get you to believe in Santa again (haha), but I do think this aspect of *The Polar Express* can be applied to the Christian journey of faith—**we're all going to face doubt**. At specific points in our journey, the voice of doubt may feel overwhelming and frightening. Sometimes, it may even seem louder than the voice of truth.

Just as the boy could not escape his feelings of doubt and had to face them head-on, so do we, as Christians. Ignoring doubt and sweeping it under the rug only means we are saving it for a later day. God asks us to be honest with Him about our doubts and to bring them to Him, just as Thomas did. Ultimately, as Jesus followers, we also have to decide to face our doubts with faith.

Read

Read John 20:24–29 again, this time focusing on the theme of **doubt** that you have already underlined in red. Did you notice how Jesus treated doubting Thomas? Describe here Jesus' heart toward Thomas.

First, I love how Jesus immediately turned toward Thomas and addressed his doubts. He told Thomas to see Him and touch Him—it was **exactly what Thomas said he needed** in order to believe. Jesus graciously met Thomas in his doubt.

Second, Jesus directly confronts Thomas' doubt by saying, "Do not disbelieve, but believe" (v. 27). He is a God of grace and directness. He confronts us and points us back to Himself when we have gone astray.

My heart is drawn to Jesus in the way He loved Thomas because I know **the same Jesus who loved Thomas through his doubts is the same Jesus who loves you and me through our doubts**.

Inward Transformation

Now, you can turn inward and reflect. In what ways have you been doubting God? Maybe, like Thomas, you have doubted Jesus' deity. Or perhaps you have lacked trust in His goodness or His ways. Journal your honest feelings of doubt, and remember that Jesus loves you, even in the midst of your questions.

Prayer

Ask Jesus to meet you in your doubts and fill you with faith. Use the prayer, "I do believe; help me overcome my unbelief!" from Mark 9:24.

Outward Application

For practical outward application, you will dive into God's Word and learn what Scripture says about your doubts. It's time to do some research. How does Scripture confront your doubts? Feel free to Google Scripture passages that are related to your area of doubt. You can look up verses for doubt, fear, trust, anxiety, faith, or suffering. Write out a verse or passage that stands out to you and helps you face your doubts.

Friend, all your doubts and questions may not have been answered today—and that's okay. If you came before the Lord and honestly told Him where you are, that is a *huge win*! In God's timing, He will meet you where you are in your doubt and fears. He will strengthen your faith!

WEEK 7 | DAY 5

Written for You to Believe

Dig Deeper

DIG DEEPER

This week, we discovered that Jesus has patience for our doubts. Whether your faith is rock solid or you are still struggling to believe, join me as we wrap up our study by digging deeper into the surrounding context of John 20:24–29 by looking at John 20:30–31.

While we focused on a number of themes in each week of this study, you may have noticed one theme that was present in them all: belief. In John 20:30–31, we clearly see belief as the focal point of John's book:

John 20:30–31

> **30** Now Jesus did many other signs in the presence of the disciples, which are not written in this book; **31** but these are written so that you may believe that Jesus is the Christ, the Son of God, and that by believing you may have life in his name.

Jesus performed thirty-five signs recorded in the four gospels,[32] with His greatest miracle being His resurrection. John hoped that people would carefully consider the signs he recorded in his book as they tried to make sense of Jesus' claims.

In these verses, John spells out the purpose of this book, which is to show people that Jesus is God's Son who came to earth in human form, and if they have faith and believe, they can receive salvation and eternal life. This passage comes right after the resurrection story in John 20:1–29, so that people can connect the purpose of believing in Jesus to the powerful narrative of His life. And it comes explicitly after the story of Thomas, who believed in Jesus only after seeing Him. John had to get the message out to people who would read his book, having never met Jesus, and he wanted them to receive the blessing of believing without seeing.[33]

What did John leave out of his gospel? See John 20:30. Use your imagination to think of other miracles Jesus might have performed. What miracles is Jesus still doing today?

In your own words write out the purpose of John's book. See John 20:31.

In what ways has believing in Jesus changed your perspective on life's challenges?

Do you feel frustrated that you can't see Jesus in person? Why do you think Jesus said, "Blessed are those who have not yet seen and yet have believed" (John 20:29)?

Reflect

How has reading the Bible changed since doing this study and learning why John wrote his gospel?

Discussion Questions

To help you reflect on the week of study, here are optional discussion questions that you can discuss with a friend, mentor, or small group.

1. How have you seen cynicism, bitterness, or doubt destroy aspects of your faith?
2. Did you notice how Jesus treats doubting Thomas? Describe Jesus' heart toward Thomas.
3. How have you struggled with doubt in the past? How have you seen God's faithfulness through that? In what ways are you struggling with doubt right now? Be honest and pray for one another.
4. In John 20:29, Jesus calls those who believe in Him without seeing Him *blessed*. What does it mean to be blessed? Read Matthew 5:3–12. How do these add to your understanding of blessedness?
5. Close your time reading 1 Peter 1:8–9 out loud. Discuss how this verse encourages you and pray through it together. Here is the verse in the format of a prayer:

   Dear Jesus, though we have not seen You, we love You. Though we do not now see You, we believe in You and rejoice with joy that is inexpressible and filled with glory, obtaining the outcome of our faith, the salvation of your souls. (1 Peter 1:8–9)

What Next?

From Ashley, Taylor, and Ellen

Congratulations, friend, on completing this seven-week study through seven major chapters in the gospel of John! We hope this study was an encouraging step that deepened your relationship with Jesus.

You may be wondering, *what's next*? We encourage you to **read the whole book of John using the EASY Bible Study Method yourself**. This method was designed for you to read and journal through the Bible independently.

Here are the steps to accomplish the EASY Method, which are the exact steps we walked you through in this study! You are already a step ahead in understanding how to study the Bible!

STEP ONE: **E – ENTER INTO THE STORY**

- Pray before reading
- Read the text slowly and thoughtfully
- Determine the context
    - Where does this fit in the storyline of the Bible?
    - Who was the original author?
    - Who was the original audience and what were they going through?
- Put yourself in the story
- Ask good questions

DIG DEEPER

- Read the text in different translations: ESV, NLT, NIV, NKJV
- When was this written? What was the date? What major events were going on during this time?
- Are there any historical or cultural things, customs, locations, or elements within the text that could be researched more in order to understand the meaning?
- What is the surrounding context of the verse or passage you are studying?
- What is the literary genre of this text and how does that add to the meaning of the passage?

STEP TWO: **A – ASSESS THE MAIN IDEA**

Paraphrase the passage in your own words

- Break up the text into chunks for summarizing into bite-size pieces and then write out a 1–2 sentence paraphrase
- Ask yourself: What is the main idea of this passage?

DIG DEEPER

- Annotate the passage (identifying keywords and themes)
    - Highlight or circle keywords and phrases, make notes of the context of the passage, ask questions, define words, connect ideas, write out your prayers, write down your honest thoughts, note God and His character
- Discover the meaning of the passage:
    - What did it mean for the original audience? Conclude in one sentence what the text meant for them in their day
    - What does it mean for us today? What are the differences and similarities you share with the original audience? Conclude in one sentence what the text means for us today
- Seek help from commentaries if necessary

STEP THREE: **S – SEEK GOD AND HIS CHARACTER**

Write out a list of who God is from the passage. "**God is ____________**"

- Find explicit qualities and characteristics of God
  - Attributes plainly written in the text
- Find implicit qualities and characteristics of God
  - Look at the context clues, mainly actions, to find attributes not plainly stated

DIG DEEPER

Meditate on God's character through

- **Prayer:** Pray over the verses, focusing on praising God for who He is
- **Journaling:** Write down your own response to God's character through means of poetry, songwriting, a letter to God, or simple journal entry
- **Art:** Meditate on Scripture and have it inspire a watercolor, collage, sketching, etc.
- **Worship:** Sing songs that proclaim the attributes you read about

STEP FOUR: **Y – YEARN FOR A HEART CHANGE AND DEEPER INTIMACY WITH GOD**

Journaling questions for inward transformation of heart and mind

- In what ways is the Holy Spirit convicting me that my heart needs to look more like God's heart?
- How does my current way of thinking need tobe challenged?
- What emotions am I feeling (e.g., fear, anxiety, bitterness) that need to be acknowledged and surrendered?
- Should I be more in awe of who God is and spend time simply praising Him for His character?
- How can a mindset shift, based on the text, change how I go about my day?

Journaling questions for outward application

- Does this text have explicit practical applications that I should follow?
- Does this text imply certain godly behaviors I should adopt as a believer?
- How can I look more like God? What practical steps can I take?
- Is this a passage that I should memorize and meditate on?

DIG DEEPER

- Create SMART goals to help you achieve your intended outcome

You can use this as a guide or download a copy to help you follow the EASY Method as you study the Bible.

If you want more detailed directions on using the EASY Method, please get a copy of *The EASY Bible Study Method* book.

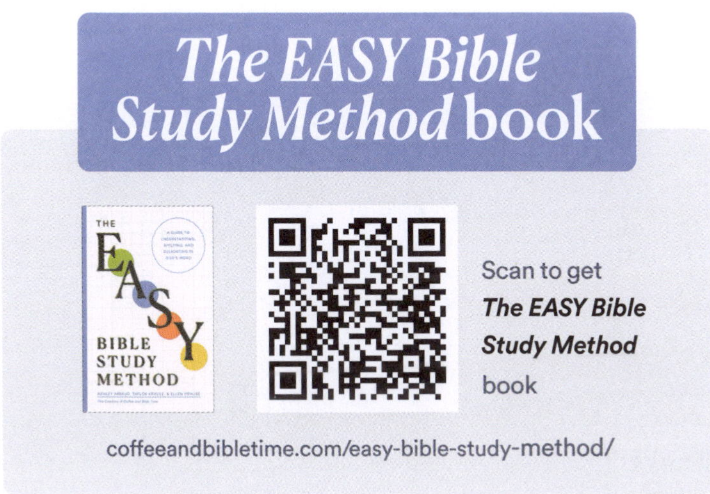

The more you study God's Word, the easier it will become. It does require time, effort, and hard work, but it's so worth it! Soon enough, studying the Bible will come naturally and easily to you through the help and power of the Holy Spirit!

Answer Key

WEEK 1

Day 2

Who is Jesus?

Jesus is God. He is the Word, the Creator, Life, and Light.

What is Jesus' mission?

Jesus' mission is to make God known (John 1:18) and to bring people into God's family (John 1:12).

John 1:9–13:

Jesus came into the world, yet, His own people rejected Him. But anyone who did believe in Him, He accepted them as His own children.

John 1:14–18:

Jesus became human and lived among people. He revealed God's glory, truth, and grace. John bore witness to Him.

Day 3

Colossians 1:15–16:

Jesus "is the **image** of the invisible God, the firstborn of all creation. For by him all things were **created**, in heaven and on earth, visible and invisible, whether thrones or dominions or rulers or authorities—all things were **created** through him and for him."

WEEK 2

Day 1

What did Jesus' disciples, such as Levi, leave behind?
Everything

Jesus instructs His disciples to love Him and place Him above what?
Family

How did Jesus tell His disciples to deny themselves?
By taking up their cross and following Him

What does Jesus tell a rich man to give up to follow Him?
All his possessions and riches, but he was not willing to give them up

Day 2

Simon Peter is introduced to Jesus by his brother Andrew. When Jesus meets Simon, he shares how he would change his name, which signifies a future identity shift through God's transformative power.

Philip is found by Jesus who asks him to follow Him. He believes Jesus to be who Moses talked about in the Old Testament. He then introduces Nathanael to Jesus.

Nathanael first hears about Jesus from Philip. He is very skeptical of Jesus coming from Nazareth. Jesus proves to Nathanael that he is deeply known and seen by Him. Nathanael believes Jesus to be the Son of God.

Main idea: John is writing to share how the first disciples were introduced to Jesus. Each of them saw that Jesus was more than just a man and that He is the Messiah. Jesus called them, and they followed.

Day 3

- Jesus is **the Lamb of God** (John 1:36)
- Jesus is **Rabbi** (John 1:38)
- Jesus is the **Messiah** (John 1:41)
- Jesus of **Nazareth** (John 1:45)
- Jesus is **the Son of God** (John 1:49)
- Jesus is **King of Israel** (John 1:49)
- Jesus is the **Son of Man** (John 1:51)

WEEK 3

Day 1

Read John 2:23–25. What does the text say happened that caused many in Jerusalem to believe?

They saw the signs that He was doing.

What sign had they just seen Jesus perform in John 2:1-11? How did the disciples respond in v. 11?

Jesus turned water into wine. His disciples believed in Him.

According to John 2:24, record why Jesus does not entrust Himself to those believers.

He knew all people.

How does this passage explain why Jesus may not have entrusted Himself to those believers?

People sometimes initially believe, but then fall away and don't bear fruit.

Look up John 7:40–52. We read that Jesus had been teaching for several days, and His words captivated the crowds. Some people had favorable opinions of Jesus, for even the temple guards had never heard anyone talk like Him. Still others became enemies. In particular, the Jewish authorities were frustrated by Jesus' rhetoric and jealous of His popularity. They

tried unsuccessfully to have Jesus arrested. How did Nicodemus respond? How was he criticized for this response?

Nicodemus advocated for a fair trial for Jesus. The Pharisees accused Nicodemus of being from the same town as Jesus, Galilee.

Look up John 19:38–42. After Jesus' crucifixion, Joseph of Arimathea received permission to take Jesus' body for burial. What did Nicodemus bring, and what did his role in the burial indicate about his view of Jesus?

Nicodemus provided seventy-five pounds of burial spices and helped Joseph wrap Jesus' body in them. He would only do this for someone he cared deeply about.

Day 2

John 3:9–15:

Jesus rebukes Nicodemus, the teacher of Israel, by telling him that if he cannot believe in earthly things, how can he believe in heavenly things?

John 3:16–21:

Because God loves us so much, He gave us his only Son to die as a substitute for our sin so that whoever believes in Him won't perish but have everlasting life. God didn't send Jesus to condemn us. The light has come into the world to overcome the darkness.

Day 3

Read the verse and draw a line to **match** it to one of the *explicit characteristics of God.*

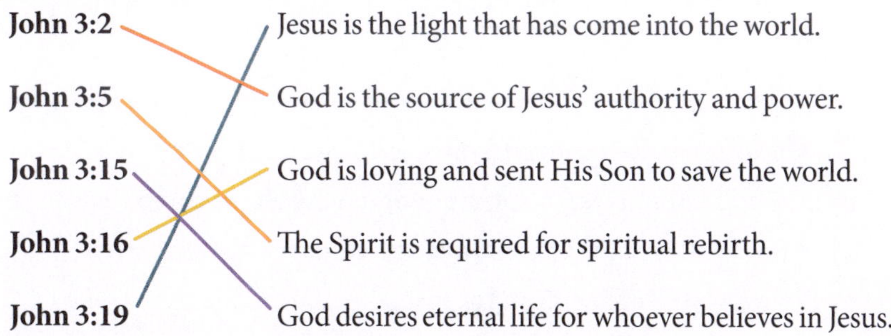

Read the verse and draw a line to **match** it to one of the *implicit characteristics of God.*

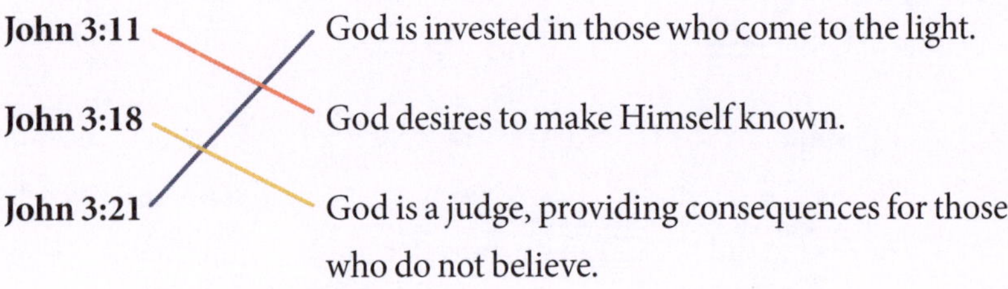

Day 4

In what ways does this passage deepen your understanding of what it means to walk in the light?
Walking in the light enhances our fellowship with God and other believers, resulting in confession and cleansing of our sins.

Based on John 3:16, what do you infer for those who do not believe?
Whoever believes in him experiences new birth (3:3, 5), has eternal life (3:15, 16), is saved (3:17); the alternative is to perish (cf. also 10:28), to lose one's life (12:25), to be doomed to destruction (17:12, cognate with 'to perish'). There is no third option.[34]

Day 5

What does the text say about God the Father?

God the Father

- Jesus comes from God
- God is with Jesus
- God's kingdom can only be seen if one is born of the Spirit
- God so loved the world that He gave His only Son
- God's intention was not to condemn the world but to save it
- God is the source of man's good works

What does the text say about God the Son?

God the Son

- Rabbi, teacher come from God, who does signs
- Declares one must be born again to see the kingdom of God
- Has ascended into heaven and descended from heaven
- Son of Man must be lifted up
- Whoever believes in Him is not condemned and has eternal life
- Whoever does not believe is condemned
- Jesus is the Light of the World
- Evil hates the light, but whoever does what is true comes to the light

What does the text say about God the Holy Spirit?

God the Holy Spirit

- Those born of the Spirit can enter the kingdom of God
- That which is born of the Spirit is spirit
- It's unknown where the Spirit comes from or where it goes

What does the text say about the Trinity?

The Trinity

- Speaks of what they know
- Bears witness to what they have seen

WEEK 4

Day 1

Read the history of the Samaritans in the text box and then look up John 4:9 and 4:27. What do you learn about ethnic and cultural divisions from the text?

There was discrimination based on religion and gender.

Well:

Source of water created by digging in the earth to find available water.[35]

Spring:

Place where water bubbles up freely from the ground.[36]

Day 2

John 4:10–15:

Jesus piques her curiosity with His dialogue, making her wonder what God's gift is, who it is that was speaking to her, and what living water is.

John 4:16–26:

Jesus exposes the truth that the woman has had five husbands. She perceives Him as a prophet and shifts the conversation from her shady past to a current religious controversy. Jesus clarifies that salvation is for the Jews because the object of their worship was known to them. Jesus continued to tell her that the hour is coming when worship is not about location. It is about worshiping the Father in spirit and truth. The woman shifts the conversation again to the Messiah, called Christ, whom she knows will come. Then Jesus boldly declares: "I who speak to you am he."

John 4:27–41:

The disciples return and marvel at why Jesus is talking with a woman. The woman leaves her water jar and tells the townspeople about Jesus. Many Samaritans from that town believe in him.

Jesus crosses ethnic, religious, and gender boundaries:
Jesus did not take part in Jewish discrimination against the Samaritans and women. He came for all.

Worshiping God in spirit and truth:
Jesus revealed that the place of worship was not what was significant. Instead, the new form of worship was Spirit-led communion with God.

Belief in Jesus:
We see the progression of the Samaritan woman's faith and ultimate belief in Jesus as the Messiah. She shared the news of Jesus with her community and many believed.

Day 3

Jesus is a **Jew** (John 4:9)
Jesus gives **living water** (John 4:10)
Jesus is a **prophet** (John 4:19)
God the Father is **worshiped in spirit and truth** (John 4:23)
God is **spirit** (John 4:24)
Jesus is the **Messiah who is called Christ** (John 4:25–26)
Jesus is **Rabbi** (John 4:31)
Jesus' mission is to **do the will of Him who sent him** (John 4:34)
Jesus is **the Savior of the world** (John 4:42)

WEEK 5

Day 1

Why was this correction necessary for the disciples to know as His representatives? Why is it essential for us to know today?
It was important for the disciples because they were Jesus' witnesses to the world. They needed to know how to navigate difficult circumstances and not simplistically attribute it to someone's sin. We need to know because we, too, are God's disciples and ambassadors today. We need to think rightly about hard topics like suffering and not blame every ailment on a person's sin.

Day 2

John 9:18–23:

The Jews question his parents and they pretend not to know anything, saying, "He is of age; ask him."

John 9:24–34:

After being questioned for the second time, the blind man is cast out for believing Jesus is from God.

John 9:35–41:

The blind man comes to faith while the Pharisees remain guilty. This is to Jesus' point: He came so that those who don't see may see, and those who do may become blind.

WEEK 6

Day 1

Having read John 10:24–39, how does it illustrate for you more vividly the love that Jesus has for Lazarus and his sisters in returning to Judea?

Going back to Judea meant facing those who had tried to stone Him to death and arrest Him. Jesus knows that He is unwanted in that area and is willing to risk His life to bring God glory, help people believe, and raise Lazarus from the dead. Jesus' love is truly self-sacrificial.

Day 2

John 11:28–37:

Jesus becomes deeply moved and weeps. Some around him question why He didn't keep Lazarus from dying.

John 11:38–44:

Despite Martha being worried about the stench of death, Jesus orders the stone to be moved away, thanks God for hearing Him, and raises Lazarus from the grave.

After paraphrasing this chapter, how do verses 25–27 stand out as particularly important? Remember that Jesus intentionally made this one of His last and most dramatic miracles before His own journey to the grave and back.

Jesus is getting to the heart of His mission and the heart of the gospel in these verses. Jesus makes it clear the <u>He</u> is the resurrection and life. Jesus is making it clear that the only way to live forever with God is to go through <u>Him</u>. There is no other way!

Day 3

Think about what you've learned in light of Jesus' response to Lazarus' death. Why is Jesus' anger acceptable while our anger needs warnings and limitations?

Our anger can very quickly become sinful, out of control, and selfish. God's anger is rooted in His character of being holy. His anger comes out when things are unjust, violate His standard of goodness, and is always righteous. We need boundaries so that we do not go out of control and grieve the Holy Spirit.

WEEK 7

Day 2

Read John 20:1–29. As you read, what main themes stick out to you from the passage?

Resurrection, new life, peace, personal encounters with Christ, belief.

John 20:24–25:

After Jesus' resurrection, many of the disciples see Jesus face-to-face—but Thomas does not. They tell Thomas about Jesus' resurrection and Thomas doubts, saying he would never believe unless He sees and touches Jesus.

John 20:26–28:

Over a week later, Jesus reappears to the disciples again, this time including Thomas. Thomas sees and touches Jesus and believes.

John 20:29:

Jesus questions Thomas for believing only after seeing. Jesus then gives a blessing to those who believe in Him without seeing Him.

John 20:29:

Jesus said to him, "Have you believed because you have seen me? Blessed are those who have not seen and yet have believed."

What does it mean to be blessed?

I like how one scholar puts it: To be blessed means that "God pours out his blessings in a special way on those who find faith even when they have no opportunity to "see" and walk with Jesus."[37]

Day 3

Reference:	Verse:	Key Insights
John 1:1	In the beginning was the Word, and the Word was with God, and the Word was God.	Jesus was in the beginning. He was with God the Father and He is God.
John 20:28	Thomas said to him, "My Lord and my God!"	Thomas declares Jesus to be his personal Lord and God.
1 John 5:20	And we know that the Son of God has come and has given us understanding, so that we may know him who is true; and we are in him who is true, in his Son Jesus Christ. He is the true God and eternal life.	God's Son came so that we may know Him. He is true, the true God, and eternal life.

Romans 9:5	To them belong the patriarchs, and from their race, according to the flesh, is the Christ, who is God over all, blessed forever. Amen.	Christ is God overall.
Titus 2:13	. . . waiting for our blessed hope, the appearing of the glory of our great God and Savior Jesus Christ,	Jesus is our great God who will return again one day.

Day 4

Did you notice how Jesus treated doubting Thomas? Describe here Jesus' heart toward Thomas.

Jesus immediately turned toward Thomas and addressed his doubts. He told Thomas to see him and touch him: exactly what Thomas said he needed (the exact same words) in order to believe. Jesus graciously met Thomas in his doubt. Jesus directly confronts Thomas' doubt by saying "Do not disbelieve, but believe." He is a God of grace and directness. He confronts us and points us back to himself when we have gone astray.

NOTES

This Bible Study Is for You

1. This quote has been widely attributed to St. Augustine, Charles Spurgeon, and Matthew Henry, though no definitive source has been identified.

Overview of the EASY Bible Study Method

2. Coffee and Bible Time, "EASY Bible Study Method!," October 25, 2024, YouTube, 8:47, https://www.youtube.com/watch?v=tN3mQG-MMGc.

Week 1 | Day 5: Believe Is a Verb

3. Grant R. Osborne, *John: Verse by Verse*, Osborne New Testament Commentaries, ed. Jeffrey Reimer et al. (Lexham Press, 2018), 31–32. Emphasis added.
4. Jeffrey J. Meyers, *Wisdom for Dissidents* (Canon Press, 2022), 94.
5. Osborne, *John*, 31–32. Emphasis added.
6. Osborne, *John*, 31–32.

Week 2 | Day 4: Come In and Stay Awhile

7. Grant R. Osborne, *John: Verse by Verse*, Osborne New Testament Commentaries, ed. Jeffrey Reimer et al. (Lexham Press, 2018), 51.

Week 3 | Day 1: Seek to Know

8. D. A. Carson, *The Gospel According to John*, The Pillar New Testament Commentary (InterVarsity, 1991), 187–88.
9. Warren W. Wiersbe, *Wiersbe Bible Commentary: New Testament* (David C. Cook, 2007), 236.
10. Carson, *The Gospel According to John*, 189.
11. James D. Price and Luder G. Whitlock, Jr. "Apostasy." In *Baker Encyclopedia of the Bible*, Vol. 1, ed. Walter A. Elwell (Baker, 1988), 130.
12. Craig S. Keener, *The IVP Bible Background Commentary: New Testament* (InterVarsity 1993), 19:38–39.

Week 3 | Day 2: Spirit, Do a Work in Me

13. Grant R. Osborne, *John: Verse by Verse*, Osborne New Testament Commentaries, ed. Jeffrey Reimer et al. (Lexham Press, 2018), 83.

Week 3 | Day 4: Walk in the Light

14. D. A. Carson, *The Gospel According to John*, The Pillar New Testament Commentary (InterVarsity, 1991), 187–88.

Week 4 | Day 1: Travel to Samaria

15. Barry J. Beitzel, *The Moody Bible Atlas* (Moody, 2025), 267.
16. Grant R. Osborne, *John: Verse by Verse*, Osborne New Testament Commentaries, ed. Jeffrey Reimer et al. (Lexham Press, 2018), 98.
17. Carson, *The Gospel According to John*, 216.
18. Carson, *The Gospel According to John*, 222.

19. Robert G. Rayburn II, "Well," in *The Lexham Bible Dictionary*, ed. John D. Barry et al. (Lexham Press, 2016); Robert G. Rayburn II, "Spring," in *The Lexham Bible Dictionary*, ed. John D. Barry et al. (Lexham Press, 2016).

Week 4 | Day 3: Run to Jesus

20. Elwell and Beitzel, "Omniscience." In *Baker Encyclopedia of the Bible*, 1588.
21. Elwell and Beitzel, "Omnipotence." In *Baker Encyclopedia of the Bible*, 1588.
22. Olivia Lane, "Woman at the Well," February 25, 2021, YouTube, https://www.youtube.com/watch?v=rnDCEe0kG6U.

Week 5 | Day 1: Healed on the Sabbath

23. John Piper, "Why Did Jesus Use Spit and Mud to Heal?," Desiring God, April 19, 2023. https://www.desiringgod.org/interviews/why-did-jesus-use-spit-and-mud-to-heal.

Week 6 | Day 3: He Was Deeply Moved

24. David Guzik, "Enduring Word Bible Commentary John Chapter 11," Enduring Word, December 10, 2015, https://enduringword.com/bible-commentary/john-11/.

Week 6 | Day 4: For God's Glory

25. John Piper, "Glorifying God . . . Period," Desiring God, July 15, 2013. https://www.desiringgod.org/messages/glorifying-god-period.

Week 6 | Day 5: Doctrine of the Resurrection

26. Warren W. Wiersbe, *Be Alive (John 1–12): Get to Know the Living Savior*, The BE Series Commentary (David C. Cook, 2009), chap. 11, EPUB.

Week 7 | Day 2: Blessed Are Those Who Believe

27. Grant R. Osborne, *John: Verse by Verse*, Osborne New Testament Commentaries, ed. Jeffrey Reimer et al. (Lexham Press, 2018), 468.
28. Osborne, *John*, 471.
29. Paraphrased from Joseph Henry Thayer, "Lord." In *Thayer's Greek-English Lexicon of the New Testament* (Hendrickson 1996), G2962.
30. Inspired by Joseph Henry Thayer, "θεός (Theos)." *In Thayer's Greek-English Lexicon of the New Testament* (Hendrickson Publishers, 1996), G2316.
31. *The Polar Express*, directed by Robert Zemeckis (Burbank, CA: Warner Bros. Pictures, 2004), DVD, 00:44:01.

Week 7 | Day 5: Written for You to Believe

32. Edwin A. Blum, "John," in *The Bible Knowledge Commentary: An Exposition of the Scriptures*, vol. 2, eds. J. F. Walvoord and R. B. Zuck (Victor Books, 1985), 344.
33. D. A. Carson, *The Gospel According to John*, The Pillar New Testament Commentary (InterVarsity, 1991), 660–61.

Answer Key

34. D. A. Carson, *The Gospel According to John*, The Pillar New Testament Commentary (InterVarsity, 1991), 206.
35. John C. H. Laughlin, "Well," in *Holman Illustrated Bible Dictionary*, ed. Chad Brand et al. (Holman, 2003), 1669.
36. "Spring," in *Holman Illustrated Bible Dictionary*, 1532.
37. Grant R. Osborne, *John: Verse by Verse*, Osborne New Testament Commentaries, ed. Jeffrey Reimer et al. (Lexham Press, 2018), 471.

Acknowledgements

All glory to God for this Bible study!

To our amazing **Coffee and Bible Time community**—thank you for being the heartbeat behind this Bible study. Your support means the world to us!

Thank you to **Moody Bible Institute** for shaping us with a rich foundation in God's Word.

To our church families at **Village Church of Gurnee** and **Calvary Church**—thank you for your constant encouragement and prayers.

Endless gratitude to our incredible publishing team: **Judy Dunagan**, **Erin Davis**, **Ashleigh Slater**, **Connor Sterchi**, **Hope Francis**, **Christianne Debysingh**, and **Janis Backing**—you made this dream a reality.

Our hearts are full. Thank you, thank you, thank you!

Connect with us!

Coffee and Bible Time

Coffee and Bible Time is a vibrant Christian ***YouTube channel*** and ***podcast*** where sisters Ashley and Taylor and their Mentor Mama, Ellen, post weekly to encourage and equip people to delight in God's Word and thrive in Christian living!

coffeeandbibletime.com

Join thousands using our resources:

- Free downloadables
- Faith-based blog
- Online shop featuring **#1 selling prayer journal**
- In-Depth Bible Study Academy
- Online community
- Uplifting newsletter
- Inspirational Instagram

MOODY PUBLISHERS
WOMEN
BIBLE STUDIES

REFRESHINGLY DEEP BIBLE STUDIES TO DWELL & DELIGHT IN GOD'S WORD

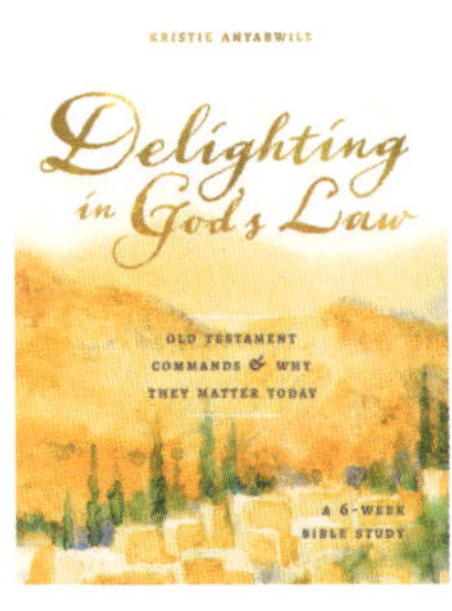

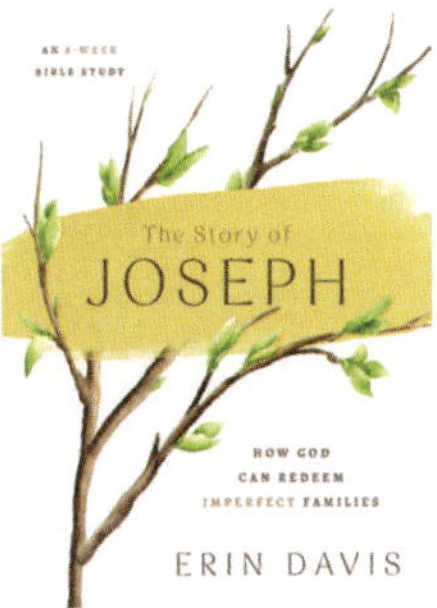

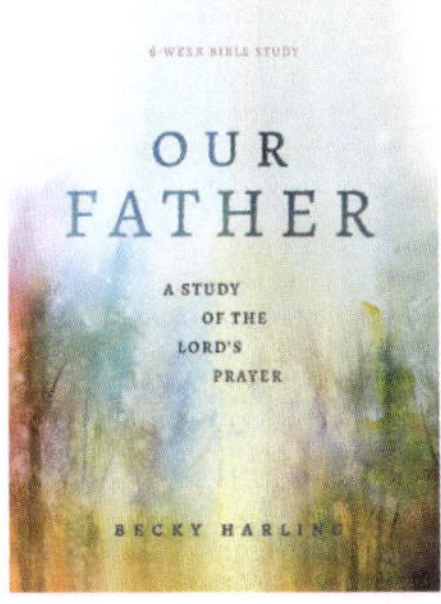

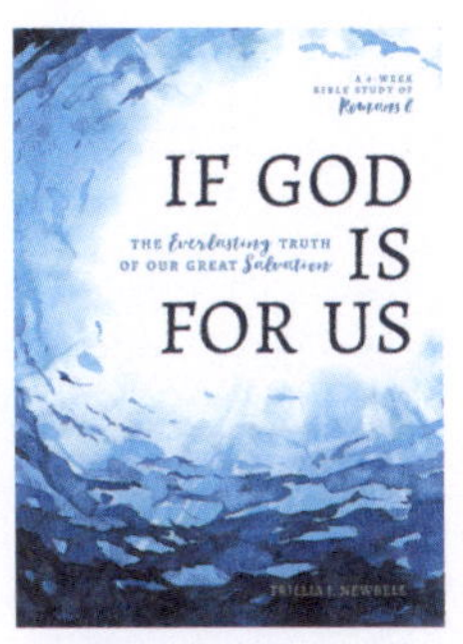

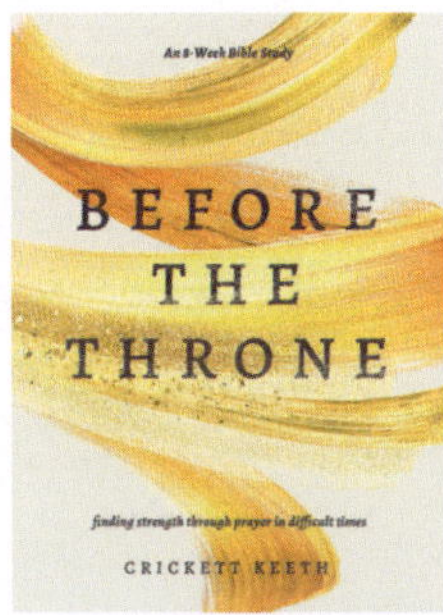

Find yours at: MoodyPublishersWomen.com